D1038163

Memphis Afternoons

BOOKS BY JAMES CONAWAY

The Big Easy

Judge: The Life and Times of Leander Perez

The Texans

World's End

The Kingdom in the Country

Napa

Memphis Afternoons

Memphis Afternoons

A MEMOIR

James Conaway

A RICHARD TODD BOOK
HOUGHTON MIFFLIN COMPANY
BOSTON / NEW YORK
1993

Library of Congress Cataloging-in-Publication Data

Conaway, James.
Memphis afternoons : a memoir / James Conaway.
p. cm.
"A Richard Todd book."
ISBN 0-395-62945-4
1. Conaway, James — Homes and haunts — Tennessee — Memphis.
2. Fathers and sons — Tennessee — Memphis — Biography. 3. Novelists, American — 20th century — Biography. 4. Memphis (Tenn.) — Social life and customs. 5. Journalists — United States — Biography.
6. Memphis (Tenn.) — Biography. I. Title.
PS3553.0486Z47 1993 92-44909
813'.54 — dc20 CIP

Printed in the United States of America

Book design by Robert Overholtzer

AGM 10 9 8 7 6 5 4 3 2 1

A portion of this book previously appeared in
Harper's Magazine in somewhat different form.

AUTHOR'S NOTE: The events in this book are as I remember them.
In a few instances names outside the family have been changed.

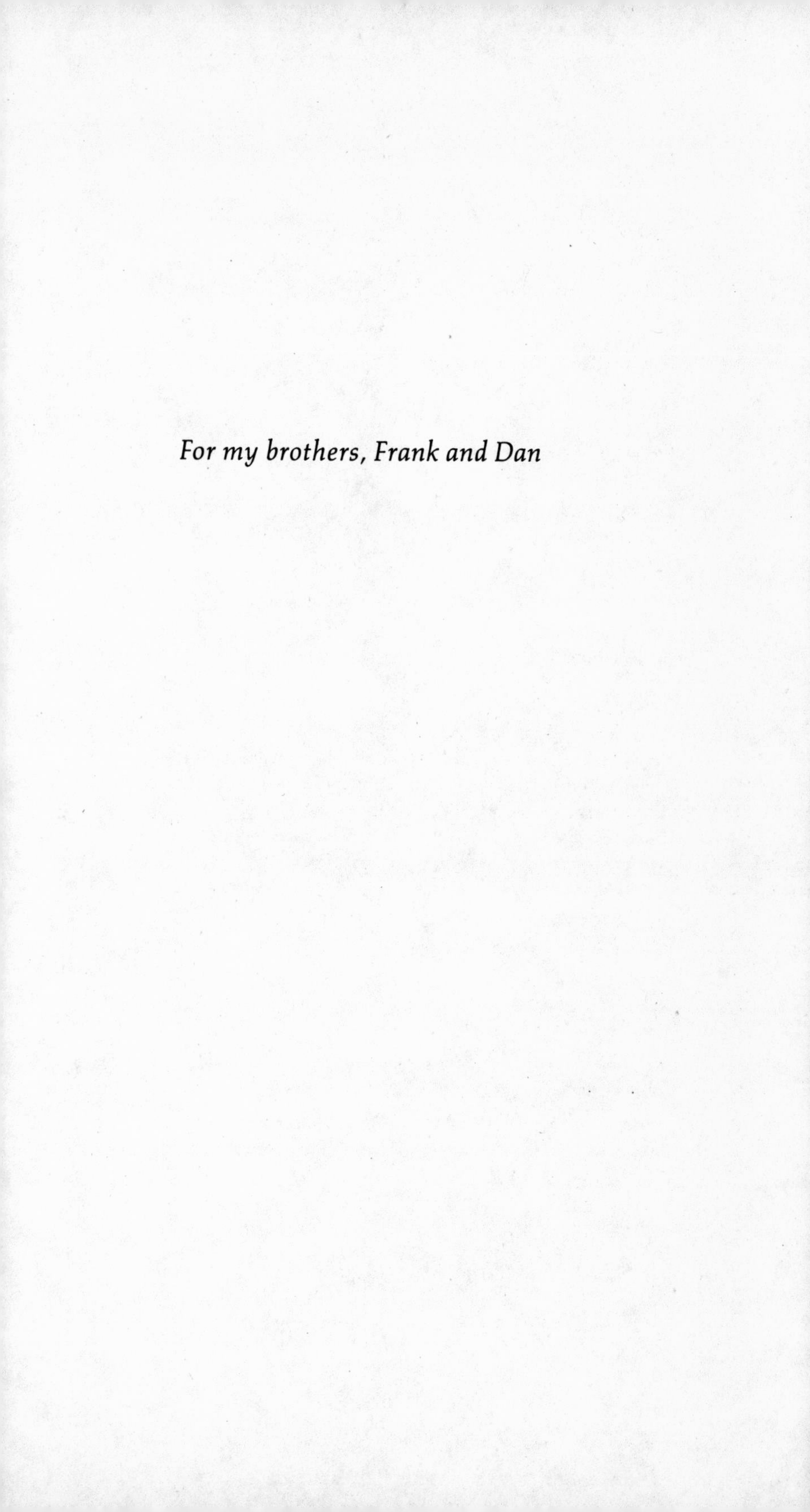

For my brothers, Frank and Dan

Memphis Afternoons

LATE AUTUMN — monsoon season. Ragged skies rolling out of Arkansas would have dropped tornadoes on a city less blessed than Memphis. I arrived in a little jet, owned by an east Tennessee bank, filled to capacity with successful dealers in estates, real and fabricated; one of these men would soon be indicted and sent to prison, but for the moment they were merrily chasing deals around the South, and I was to write about them for the *Washington Post*, my employer at the time.

This part of America was so different from what I had left behind as to seem irrelevant. That the Deep South is another world has often been observed, but the fact that it remained so struck me, once again, as remarkable. I had grown up in Memphis and had been going back for more than twenty years. Much had happened since I had left for good, in the sixties, and yet Memphis retained its palpable otherness. But some of the anomalies of time and place persisted in the mind of the displaced adult I had become, one who was married, solvent, and recognizable by profession. My wife and children had remained in Washington this time, as they often did when

I returned "home," an event with a familiar pattern: anticipation fractured by present reality and the unfulfilled promises of childhood, vague but tenacious, and the observation that home has not been sufficiently chastened by one's absence. Returning, I had always felt the poignancy of time passing, a comfortable melancholy full of the evidence of my own lengthening existence, but I had reached the point where the self-congratulation I felt at surviving would be replaced by an entirely different emotion.

My father waited on the street where the bankers' limousine left me, sitting at the wheel of his small car. I knew immediately that something was wrong. The face beneath the snap-brim hat seemed diminished, the eyes full of misgiving. The neighborhood should have been familiar territory but he regarded it as alien.

"Hello, sonny boy," he said when I got in.

I put my arm around his shoulders and gave him an awkward kiss on the cheek, not common practice among males in my family — men don't kiss each other — but in this sad, befuddled moment I felt bound to console him. In truth, I had known for years that my father was slowly losing his mind, had seen the signs spread across the sheets of graph paper on which he, an engineer, occasionally wrote to me in a hand so crabbed that the letters grew increasingly brief, and finally ceased. I had accepted this and his hesitancy on the telephone, his difficulty with numbers — for years he had calculated how much refrigerated air Memphis's buildings need to remain habitable — and his slight stammer as the mental perambulations of an independent old man who lived within the bounds of propriety and had known some disappointment and hardship. I should have put off the concerns of my own life and thought more about these little routine absences that would lead inexorably to a larger one.

Dad wore the shoes he always wore for yard work, of rough

suede darkened by contact with dead leaves that in the fall became his preoccupation, moved from beneath the canopy of trees to the curb. I could — still can — see the slightly stooped figure in windbreaker and khakis, the brisk strokes, the pauses to reckon the size and grudging direction of his load. Raking was one metaphor for Dad's life and not necessarily an unhappy one, since he enjoyed work and the supply of leaves was inexhaustible.

He drove without talking, concentrating on the task at hand, running a stop sign, turning a corner without regard for the oblique stream of oncoming traffic or horn blasts, passing a pedestrian who wisely decided not to challenge our passage because otherwise he would have been killed, not by the violence of the initial blow but by the car's dogged persistence in running him over. Dad, it seemed, did not intend to stop until he had returned to the shelter of the car port, attached to a house that had been sleek and modern in the sixties, when he and my mother bought it, set back among the mass of trees and shrubs that precipitate Memphis's botanical exuberance every spring. That November, the house seemed enfolded in drenched, near-tropical profusion.

My mother met us at the door in bathrobe and slippers — the uniform, since looking after my father had become a constant endeavor. Together we got him out of his hat and raincoat and seated on the low couch in the living room, where he watched the evening news on television without interest. When Mom and I were alone, I said angrily, "He shouldn't be driving," and she said, "It's all he's got left."

My father's life was as different from mine as were our aspirations and our selves, but the past was mostly a common one. From that point on it required a kind of dead reckoning. I and the rest of my family were for the foreseeable future caught up in Dad's misfortune, but eventually I would realize that the questions I had meant to ask him wouldn't be answered, that the stories and rumors I had absorbed as a child, scoffed at as an adolescent, and wanted more of as an adult were in a sense lost. In many instances I would never know where the actual left off and the amends began, and by that time it would matter more than I had thought possible.

Most of what I knew of my family came directly from them, and from letters and photographs that act as much as light to the inner eye as absolute delineators of what people looked like and did. I would decide, years later, to fill in a bit — a version of the examined life. Much of this life belonged to others but remained tangentially mine. Even so, such a venture could easily founder, for there are reasons for what went before, freighted with every protective interpretation between past and present.

I know now that reality must be, at least in part, imaginary. Like any fond or desperate family involvement, this one had no frontiers; the more I looked, the more I wondered. About perceptions, theirs and mine. About what they had chosen to tell me, and each other, and what we all chose to forget.

1

HE WAS KNOWN as Connie and he decided to fight the Japanese when I was two. I don't remember the day he left but I do remember the end of his first leave: hot metal stairs leading up to a railway platform in midtown, my father's smooth cheeks and shining summer dress uniform, the hat emblazoned with a gold eagle as he leans out the door of the departing train, an immaculate white wedge, smiling unhappily, one hand raised as if testing the wind.

He didn't have to enlist in the United States Navy, being too old for the draft; my mother never forgave him. As a Seabee he fought alongside the Marines on Peleliu and came back to Memphis full of stories of air raids and a sun hotter than the one at home; of tropical birds that flew backward; of an enemy that holed up in caves and floated face-down, dead, in mountain pools or that appeared at dawn, naked, uniforms neatly bundled and placed with their weapons at a distance while they balanced on rocks, surrendering. At least some of the stories were buttressed with hardware: a knife made from a Japanese aircraft, glass balls that had washed up on the beaches which had held afloat the fishing nets of other yellow people on that far ocean. Nothing reinforced the exotic quality of my father's war more than those smooth, green globes, the smoky glass full of bubbles and strange imperfections.

My mother's anxieties, love, and resentment were poured out in letters he brought back and she kept, along with his replies, wrapped in ribbon in a box on the closet floor. He joined us after the war in the house of his mother-in-law and her new husband, where work became the closest thing to having fun, a bulwark against a future that stretched unavoidably before him. Dad painted and built fences, installed a bathroom upstairs and a huge attic fan that sucked moths flat against the screens. These projects blended into a continuum decades long. I was pressed into helping when my older brother, Frank, managed to escape. "Jimbo, would you like to bring me that hammer?" Dad would say. "Jimbo, would you like to run over there and get me that board?" "Jimbo, would you like to crawl up under there and see if you can find that goddamn roll of electrical tape?"

In the process I learned journeyman carpentry: hold the hammer handle by the end, not the middle; blunt the point of a nail to prevent the board from splitting; reset screws with broken matchsticks. Sawing, cut also on the pull. Use the level to affirm what the eye has already determined. I glimpsed in the intentness of Dad's gaze and the alacrity of his thin, muscular hands the value of such skills and the satisfaction, mostly solitary, that they brought. Also a kind of control, or the illusion of it. I heard in his murmured, monumental impatience an unease that lay behind domestic compliance. I didn't know then that other men were out playing golf, shooting ducks, trolling for smallmouth bass, playing cards, and doing the other things men did on weekends.

Much has been written about whiskey in the South. It was often talked about when I was growing up, and used at odd moments. Frank once heard our uncle, in the alcoholic blush of Christmas, cradling fifths of his two favorite bourbons, proclaim to all present, "These are the standards!" The idea was that good things followed if you knew what and how to drink, and kept in practice. Boys going off for the first time to Ole Miss or UT or Chapel Hill took with them an intimate knowledge of the mysteries of drink and were known for it. Dad traveled with a quart of sour mash and he kept one in the desk drawer at his office and another in the cabinet above the refrigerator. I often saw him extract and uncork a bottle on a tedious afternoon, an act that required neither apology nor explanation. The effect was palpably mellow, even to a boy looking on, a pleasant lengthening of Dad's self-imposed deadlines, a softening of the hot Memphis light that infiltrated his offices.

Alcohol had a strange effect upon adults, heightening their color and drawing out their already long vowels. It made them laugh too much, or not enough. One night my parents returned from a party with Dad transformed: he swayed, and his face reflected a tight distortion I associated with a misplaced T-square or a banged thumb. He seemed angry but also distracted, an unusual combination. His words came in clots, and they frightened me and made me realize that to love and respect someone is not necessarily the same thing as to know him.

Already apprehensive by nature, I took this and other things more to heart than I should have; at the same time I was willful and sometimes contemptuous of adults including, on occasion, my father. I thought I saw in their habits and frivolity an opportunity for escape. What I often found was trouble, after breaking things to test their durability or traipsing in forbidden territory. Discipline imposed in whiskey time had about it a disturbing randomness.

One night Dad came to my room smelling of cigarettes and the sweet decay of bourbon. He sat on the edge of the bed and gently stroked my hair, unable to put into words whatever it was he had in mind. I wanted to help him but of course couldn't; I felt, I think, some of his abiding fatalism without knowing exactly what that might be.

There were verities — the sanctity of a person's word, a prompt response to bullies — that comforted me even when I didn't observe them. Connie's world was absolute: Don't put on airs. Don't take any guff. Always walk between a lady and the traffic. Respect machines. Do things the hard way. A man should know all this without having to be told, and if he had to be told, it was too late.

"Nuts" was the generic condemnation, a resonant bit of disdain for excuses and pretensions. Connie used a needly humor that was common currency among his few close friends. The delivery was droll, casually deprecatory. The victim was made to look like a kid, synonymous with being a dope. "I guess we'll have to help him . . ." — get a job done, find a date, zip up his pants, all this to an imaginary onlooker. Or, "The poor guy's confused" because of some show of indecision. "Oh, lovely" was an indirect, combined assault upon fancy language, privilege, or the mere suggestion of feminine sensibility in a male.

Even new acquaintances were subjected to a not-so-gentle devaluation. Dad was pleased by a similar retort at his expense. Yet he rarely used that kind of humor on me and would have been annoyed if my jokes had cut into his self-esteem. Rather, we made fun of each other through objects, and other people, that didn't perform as they were supposed to. We laughed at absurdities that for some reason weren't always obvious to others. We didn't argue directly, then or later, but simply stated our views, as if the arbitrator stood by, weighing all this.

Dad was both anti-establishment and traditional, populist

and conservative, approving of Andrew Jackson, for instance, because he reportedly spat a mouthful of hot potatoes onto White House linen, yet envying Britain its monarchy. Memphis was his city. Its comfortable, absolute certitudes ultimately became for me a symbol of the nation's complacency, but Dad didn't feel that way. He took pleasure in the city's growth, suggesting that Memphis would become part of the "mainstream" even as it gave up the quirkiness that made it interesting and so southern.

Sometimes the heroic and the preposterous came together in a meld of good will and whiskey that embarrassed me. For a time I reluctantly brought friends to our house, not because Dad was abusive but because he drank too much and because his tales — his being — seemed outlandish. He belonged to another time and had too many opinions, yet my friends talked to and even courted him. Their fathers were generally more successful, and diplomatic when they weren't pious; their restraint increased the distance between them and me and my friends, but Dad was always willing — sometimes too willing — to say what was on his mind. And making a similar, absolute assertion in his presence, no matter what the subject, got an immediate response.

Dad claimed, among other things, that William Faulkner spent most of his waking hours in a tree, that long baths could kill you, and that an uncle of his had knocked a mule unconscious in the Hunt Berlin coal yard on Central Avenue. More difficult for me to accept was the response of the other sex. Girls listened and laughed, as polite people did, and Memphians are polite, but they also clearly *liked* my father. After I was grown, a young woman said to me, in my parents' living room, a glass of scotch in her hand and on her face the smile of the recently snowed, "You know, your father's sexy." I wondered just what she meant.

I never once heard him sing.

2

MY FIRST, dim notion of a past was embodied not in the house where I grew up but in a gray stone one in midtown, once the eastern extremity of Memphis, full of stolid residences with alleys behind garages that had been stables, and big trees casting shade over a capacious, humane self-satisfaction. Dad's family rose out of that place, aspiring burghers by virtue of a fierce one-legged Confederate veteran who had owned property close to what became Overton Park. My grandmother, great-aunt, and great-uncle all lived together there, with hard horsehair furniture and on the hearth an oriental vase of mesmerizing fragility.

They received us every Sunday for dinner, a Wagnerian event that occurred shortly after noon; I was told that they had dressed my father up in girls' clothes when he was a child, to satisfy some Victorian urge no one could explain to me at age four, or at forty. I was determined that they were not going to do it to me. Dad had also been given a walking stick; at five or six, on special occasions, he would board the elevator in the Peabody Hotel wearing his dress, flourishing his cane, and puffing on a cigarette filled with an herbal concoction.

Dresses on boys weren't as common in the teens of this century as at the end of the last one, but the custom had held on in Overton Park.

Dad's mother, the former Willie Mae Rudisill, poured the contents of her chamber pot on the roses in the back yard, or so I was told. I remember a reserve in her that in retrospect seems barely southern. The Rudisills had come indirectly from Holland to rural Tennessee and progressed from farming to selling coal and chinaware. Her husband, Idee Conaway, was a traveling salesman. I never knew him. The photographs of Idee show a black Irishman who put on weight and lost his hair; the soulful eyes were passed on to my father, but not the girth. Dad spoke proudly of his father teaching him eight-ball and rotation in darkling pool halls from St. Louis to Jackson, stops on his route as a drummer, and I sometimes wonder what other part of his father my father replicated.

Dad's brother, Edwin, sixteen years older, had functions more paternal than fraternal. All I remember of him is a kind of windiness when he entered a room. As the younger brother to this bluff, funny entrepreneur, my father had grown up believing in the successful enterprise. Edwin had introduced ice to the mid-South, bringing the ice house to rural extremities — barns with sweaty oak doors opening into the murk, hung with sides of beef and ham haunches, stacked with blue-green slabs of ice giving off fog in layers that crept along the floors and spilled over the thresholds. They were money machines, and Edwin used them to build a small fortune in stocks.

My father had seemed destined to get rich through ice, too. First he went off to Washington and Lee, in Virginia, as good southerners did, with Edwin paying his way. But while in Lexington, Dad received word that Edwin and his ice houses were in trouble — the 1929 crash had caught him — and their lives took different turns. Dad left W & L to pursue something practical; years later, Edwin, driving at night along a two-lane highway far from Memphis, trying to revive his fortune, met on the downward slope of a hill a sedan driven by a drunk on the wrong side of the line.

The telescope directed backward cuts through life, eliminating the sidelines where children stand. For them there is only the present, the vast fabric of Now, frayed at the edges by the peculiar behavior of adults. I remember the call coming in, and my mother's cry of pain. My brother and I looked at each other, and we laughed, not because the news was funny but because we could tell, in that moment of crisis, that no one knew what to do.

My father's mother and his aunt Mamie, a spinster and already a bit loony when I knew her, wear high-necked gowns in the photographs in the oval frames. I still see them that way, rather than in the loosely fitted seersucker dresses better suited to Memphis in July. They were inscrutable, though kind, with no clear connection to my father. The orderliness of their domain intimidated me. I know now that it mightily impressed my father, too, that his personal fastidiousness and innocent obsessions, like the drawers he made in later life out of Philadelphia Cream Cheese boxes to segregate nuts and bolts by size, were rooted in Overton Park.

It was his uncle Yank that my father most clearly admired. His name, like my father's, was Frank; the nickname, a childish mispronunciation, was appropriate because it suggested violent displacement. Yank wore a dark suit even in the worst Memphis heat and a black hat with a round brim that shaded his blue, blue eyes. The suits obscured a ropy muscularity on a short frame but not the big, misshapen hands. He did not seem capable of once having carried a hogshead full of flour down his cellar stairs, but my father claimed to have seen it.

From Yank I first heard the word "ruckus" — something that transpired among men in Memphis, in far-off, crepuscular time. No matter how innocently Yank's stories began, they all ended in a ruckus. Sitting in the living room, coat off, armbands squeezing his biceps, his black, high-topped shoes aligned, Yank would talk, with prompting, of Boss Crump's voting frauds, of misbehavior at the racetrack, and encounters in Pinch, the poor Irish section down by the river that became a black one. All human intercourse led to conflict, and somehow Yank was always drawn in. The stories ended shy of the first blow, but the sight of Yank's bony, distended knuckles was resolution enough.

There were other stories, told by my father when Yank wasn't present: Yank felling the mule in the coal yard where he worked; Yank knocking a man through Sears, Roebuck's plate glass; Yank fighting his way out of an alley off Beale Street where he had sought refuge from ruffians and discovered a barrel full of empty whiskey bottles.

The coal yard was owned by Yank and his brother, June, a Chamber of Commerce stalwart who lived just blocks away. Yank collected due bills for deliveries in Pinch. As a young man he had strolled between taverns with his pockets stuffed with cash, armed only with a roll of dimes in each fist. Dad had seen him step down from the trolley in the evenings and spit his plug of chewing tobacco against the curb. His sisters did not approve of tobacco, and on those rare evenings when Yank forgot to spit, he would sit in the parlor until his sisters looked the other way, then tip the oriental vase toward him and deliver his quid into its maw.

Yank gave my brother and me sacks of pennies dumped onto his bachelor's bureau at night. In those piles of gratuitous copper winked nickel and silver; we would count the coins and pack them into wrappers to be traded at the bank for folding money. Before Sunday dinner Yank would escort us to the zoo, where we rode the diminutive ferris wheel and the merry-go-round while he stood by; I remember a feeling of absolute security: we could revolve endlessly beneath the white Memphis sky, eat a river of popcorn, and thrust our faces through the head-holes in the photographer's Wild West backdrop until the film ran out. Finally Yank would consult the pocket watch with the faded green numerals and coal dust under the lens, and lead us back to the house.

My father once saw him racing through town at night in a red buggy, standing behind his mares, on his way to meet a woman no one in his family acknowledged. That must have been in the twenties. Memphis was a sensual place then. The river still brought islands of hardwood and other marketables. Cotton reigned and the commerce of Front Street added to the welter of downtown life. Beale oozed a new, illicit sound while pumping the smells of fried catfish and pulled-pig barbecue into close summer nights. There were visiting operas, and musicales. You could buy locally rolled nickel cigars near Whiskey Chute. Whores hung out the windows along Vance and other downtown thoroughfares, and heroin was delivered on bicycles.

My brother would someday write a short story about Yank, his sisters, and Yank's lover that captures them well. Reading it, I am reminded that Yank sometimes fell asleep with one eye open, that Mamie put out milk for the dead. I think the big painting in the entrance hall struck my brother, too, as the embodiment of Yank's longing, the "young lady whose feet were wrapped in thorns and whose hand lifted delicately after some pregnant fruit," an acceptable substitute for an opera singer he loved, in a diaphanous gown.

Frank described Yank's singer as "poutingly beautiful, fragile, sallow-faced." Also Italian, which meant Catholic, difficult encounters for Yank when simply walking down the street.

The hapless fellow he knocked through the plate glass window was Catholic, knocked through *because* he was Catholic, or at least because Yank suspected it. Love may have been stronger than prejudice, but because the singer was not acceptable to his sisters, Yank declined to marry her.

We watched Yank's fortunes decline while those of brother June improved. Charming, circumspect, demonstrably Christian, June danced with his wife at the Peabody and regularly appeared in the *Commercial Appeal* as a promulgator of good works. He wore spectacles with gold rims and three-piece suits better tailored than Yank's, his watch attached to a gold chain that luxuriously draped the prominent stomach. I remember his tight vest straining the buttonholes, when I was ten or eleven, and the jokes and incomprehensible asides that made me laugh and wish for more. We are standing on the steps outside a mansion on Poplar Avenue converted to a retirement home, the last resort first for Mamie, then for my father's mother. The spectacle that awaits me inside will render subsequent Sunday afternoons depressing, associated with the reek of urine and the measured, bleary-eyed desperation of trapped old people for whom I feel vague responsibility.

Yank's business sense had never been the best. When he was offered stock in a bold new company called Coca-Cola, he rejected it, saying, "The world will always need coal. This is just fizz." His favorite phrase, "You're wrong about that," was applied to any assertion striking him as presumptuous, and most did. He had no use for experts or self-appointed authorities, thrived on a kind of homegrown anarchy, an amiable know-nothingism that accepted no bounds abroad from the house and no license within it. "You're wrong about that" must have brought on many a ruckus in the moil of old downtown Memphis.

3

My mother's family had more influence on my father than his own, on all of us in fact. It came relatively early and lasted almost to the time Dad fell ill, a powerful matriarchal melody over the strident sounds of the present that I heard long before I knew where it came from. It would take most of my lifetime to understand, but I recognized the components of a good if carefully censored libretto, with characters — some dead, some immortal — who indirectly shaped my father, and consequently me.

Mom often showed me sketches kept in a big folder in a closet in the "studio" behind the house in which I grew up — not the sleek car-ported rancher my parents later bought, not the house in Overton Park, but a red brick bungalow under spreading oaks on Highland Avenue, with a swing on chains at the end of a white-columned porch. Mom would say, in a serene voice, "Your grandfather drew these." They were of Hambone, a poor black man; the words in the balloons made no sense to me, but Hambone's round cheeks, rheumy eyes, and shining forehead had a tactile reality, since the lead engravings of the cartoons lay about the studio, along with other evidence of my grandfather's craft: scarred drawing board, long-handled pens with elaborate brass nibs, pots of glossy black India ink, yellow cardboard, and over all the congruent smells of pencil shavings and tobacco.

I was told that my grandfather, J. P. Alley, had been the syndicated political cartoonist for the *Commercial Appeal* and winner of a Pulitzer back in the twenties. But he had been made famous in the South by Hambone, who delivered himself of homespun truths on subjects as various as warfare and women's hats in a dialect so tortured that Uncle Remus sounds glib by comparison. Why, I wondered, had this character been created by a white man whose photograph I saw in the album, with severely parted hair and an intense gaze no child could be comfortable with?

I never knew my grandfather, and didn't regret it as much as I should have, according to my mother. Her love for him was frightening in its intensity. I wish now I had been more understanding when she spoke of him as a collapsed bridge between herself and what was meaningful and satisfying in life, and more appreciative of a talent that took him all over the country, even to Hollywood.

It's all there, in the photographs. The one of J. P. Alley and the movie director King Vidor shows them standing outside a production studio. My grandfather had gone to Hollywood to discuss the possibility of making a movie about Hambone. It is the cartoonist, however, who looks the big shot in wide-brimmed hat, suit and tie, a cigar in one hand and in the other a drawing of his creation ("Law me!" says Hambone. "Mistah Vidor oughter let me in dat picture ef he wanter heah 'Hallelujah'!"). Vidor, his director's whistle on a chain around his neck, stands off to one side and regards my grandfather bemusedly, as if he can't figure out who this man is or where he came from.

*

He came from Arkansas, beyond the rice flats and white-flecked seas of cotton, the son of a preacher out of subsistence farmers and westering migrants, one of them a slaver, according to my uncle. Somewhere in the transition from southwestern Virginia to Arkansas, an Alley trafficked not in Negroes but in Indians, selling them, I suppose, to ambitious middle Tennessee pig farmers. My great-grandfather, John Pinkney Alley, served in Colquitt's 1st Regiment of the Arkansas Infantry during the Civil War, was captured by Union forces, and spent time in military prison before becoming a circuit-riding Methodist.

His son, James Pinkney Alley, my grandfather, was only six when his father died. The Alleys may have been kin to a signer of the Constitution but they had little more money than impoverished rural blacks around them, and as a young man, Jim Alley went to Little Rock to clerk in what is described in a posthumous tribute to him as a plantation supply store: "During these days, the shambling, typically thriftless darkey of the old South was a familiar figure to him," and already a cliché that would have its apotheosis in Hambone.

Jim Alley argued with his employer — "I got mad," he later wrote, with characteristic lack of amplification — and quit. Determined to be an illustrator, an unusual, some said worthless, profession, he was broke when a friend of his father's lent him money for an art correspondence course. He had by then fallen in love with the daughter of a Pine Bluff architect and builder, Nona Buchanan Lane — he called her Dodo — whose life had outshown his. Her father had driven her and her mother west in a wagon, in the first year of the century, after a doctor advised that the trip would cure his wife's tuberculosis; the Trail of Tears was as close to my grandmother-to-be's origins as the vaunted plantation South, but when her mother died in Colorado, father and daughter returned to Arkansas.

Dodo was the only student at Henderson College, in Arkadelphia, who had shot a cigar out of her father's mouth — in the presence of Frank James. The photograph of her small graduation class shows her as a serious, black-eyed young woman whose dark, gathered hair is tied at the nape of her neck and whose handsome nose is large and probably Indian. "My Most Dearest Darling," Jim Alley wrote to her in the summer of 1908, ". . . I don't know what to say or how I should say what I ought to say, but I'm going to follow this pen anyhow!" He was an angular young man with those high, flat cheekbones usually associated with sharecroppers or, farther west, bronc busters and farriers, not aspiring illustrators, and he had a temper. Dodo replied in a fine, strong hand that his trust was "that which I prize most highly of all things in my life," and they were married a year later, a Lane and an Alley, powerful suggestions of transition that no one in my family ever noticed.

My grandfather got a job with an engraving company in Memphis and undertook the adventure of moving to a city that in 1909 was a curious blend of the sanctimonious and the murderous. The mayor, Ed "Boss" Crump, also a transplant, from rural Mississippi, set about cleaning up the city while contributing to the corruption of the political process. Many voters supporting him were either dead or fanciful; wagonloads of black men were delivered to the polls, then driven to a back street to change clothes and identities, to be delivered again, all good material for a skinny young political satirist who met the editor of the *Commercial Appeal* and began drawing cartoons for the newspaper.

My grandfather's early drawings reflect the style of cartoonists of the period, with many characters and visual tropes, his rendered in a broad, impressionistic hand. He pared down the number of players and concentrated on one idea, with the diminutive Hambone on the periphery, commenting on the actions of his white betters. Soon J. P. Alley had an office at the newspaper, and Hambone earned a single-column space of his own in 1915. "I'se sorry fuh de man whut have to alluz keep laughin' to hol' he job — I laks to git mad en ac' nach'ul now en den . . ."

The young Arkansan insisted that his political cartoons, not Hambone, mattered. In 1922 the *Commercial Appeal* began carrying stories concerning a Ku Klux Klan murder in northern Louisiana. The nativist reincarnation of the Klan established during Reconstruction was on the rise; its several million members in the South and Midwest included Memphis's chief of police. The Klan killing competed on the *Commercial Appeal*'s front page with Memphis's own shootings and knifings. The newspaper's cartoonist mostly drew pictures of corrupt foreign dictators and hapless President Harding, but he occasionally criticized hooded figures in grubby robes. In 1923, to his and most everyone's surprise, the Pulitzer committee awarded the *Commercial Appeal* a prize for "its courageous attitude in the publication of cartoons and the handling of news in reference to the operations of the Ku Klux Klan." Suddenly J. P. Alley was a celebrity.

Winning a Pulitzer in Memphis could be complicated. Pulitzers were often given to those who criticized, and many people thought there was no need for criticism. If events or lives went awry, that was unfortunate. Existence entailed difficulties for which you were not accountable. The pressures of life produced sad, even tragic results, but there was nothing necessarily *wrong*. To suggest that Klansmen had an imperfect appreciation of the rules of jurisprudence was to invite Yankees with funny names to take advantage of the situation and award a prize for disloyalty. The Civil War — the War of Northern Aggression — was still a vivid reality for some people, my grandmother included. The mere existence of Yankees was a difficult proposition for her. Though certainly a foe of the Klan, Dodo held northerners responsible for the sorry state of the South and looked upon Abraham Lincoln as a traitor. Once, when I asked her what was wrong with Yankees, she said, "They put sugar on their meat." Anyone so stupid wouldn't know who deserved a prize.

As children, we were never shown the Klan cartoons, probably because they had been given away — part of my grandfather's casual largess. Consequently I thought of him first as a curiosity and then, based upon Hambone only, as a racist mugwump. Not until I was grown did I encounter, in the Library of Congress, the sketch of a hooded figure sitting on a stump with a book entitled *Law Enforcement* open on his lap, over the caption "Better read it very carefully." It didn't seem particularly courageous, but the cartoon did pose the possibility of physical harm to my grandfather and throws a weak light on the man himself.

During the 1924 presidential contest between Calvin Coolidge and John W. Davis, J.P. drew a cartoon showing a Republican elephant singing "O, we ain' gwine steal no mo'" and a Democratic donkey responding "But how'n the 'ell kin the country tell — 'You ain' gwine steal no mo'?'" that the Democratic National Committee reproduced above the entrance to its national headquarters. J. P. Alley's work began to appear in *Literary Digest* and *Review of Reviews.* Southern congressmen clipped his cartoons and posted them above the marble mantel in the Democrats' cloakroom in Washington.

Job offers from newspapers and magazines in other parts of the country apparently didn't tempt him. Jim Alley liked living in Memphis. A minister visiting the *Commercial Appeal* at the time wrote a description of J. P. Alley's office that was later published: ". . . its door ajar revealing a large window opening on Court Street; a much used flat-top desk, a straw hat and a blue summer coat sharing the same nail . . . yes, and a rose pinned on the lapel." Turner Catledge, future managing editor of the *New York Times*, then a reporter in Memphis, described the cartoonist as "ever a gentleman" who would sketch lightly with a Venus 4B pencil and then bear down in ink with free strokes. Finished, the cartoonist would stride out of his cubicle with the product in hand, bound for the engraver's and, subsequently, the golf course.

His house, designed by Dodo's father, stood then several miles east of the city limits. The studio out back served the artist's convenience while Dodo looked after two girls and two boys; life on Highland Avenue acquired a certain easefulness. My grandfather pursued the question of roots, never of much interest to the family in Arkansas, and somehow he acquired the address of Alleys in Norfolk, England. He kept a letterhead on which was printed the Alley crest: two laurel boughs adorning a crown, and the words *Nunc nunc*, which, roughly translated, meant "right now" — not the best motto for a southerner.

He and Dodo had their differences. "That's not the way I remember it, Jim," she would say when he told a funny story at someone's dinner table. She acquiesced in his success but in some basic way remained unmalleable. She read poetry aloud with friends from the West Tennessee Normal College, so close to Highland. "She helped me dream my early dreams and helped me realize my later realization," her husband told an interviewer in the fullness of his career. ". . . Could anything be better for a man than to have someone right close to him criticize him?"

When Jim Alley played poker he would drink too much, announce "I'm drunk," and one of his friends would have to drive him home. My grandmother later spoke with resignation of her husband, the son of a Methodist minister, the gentleman with the rose in his lapel, the acknowledged vessel of regional wit, not being able to hold his liquor. Memphis was officially dry but drinking remained the most popular indoor sport. Crump was subsequently removed from the mayor's office by the state supreme court for failing to enforce Tennessee's anti-drinking laws, rather than for his blatant voting frauds. (He simply became a county official instead of a city one, and kept his control intact.) According to a history of the *Commercial Appeal*, he stopped by Alley's office in the midst of some political turmoil and told my grandfather, "Jim, you're bearing down pretty heavy. You're killing me." My grandfather said, "Well, dammit, Ed, behave yourself."

The exchange, if factual, reflects the avuncular nature J. P. Alley was famous for, but the reverse side of his character asserted itself as often. Memphis's favorite cartoonist and Memphis's most powerful man often attended the same business luncheons; once, when my grandfather was to speak, Crump telephoned him to say that if my grandfather got drunk beforehand, he was to call and Crump would send a car for him. Sometime before lunch my grandfather did call, told Crump "I'm drunk," and hung up. He never appeared at the podium.

During Prohibition, my grandfather used Memphis's speakeasies; at least once he broke furniture. "He wasn't the tea-drinking type," says my uncle, J.P.'s son-in-law. We are sitting in a revolving restaurant on the top of a bank building with a cycloramic view of the Mississippi, talking about the past. My uncle is an old man now, telling stories about J. P. Alley, long gone, that could not be told in the presence of either my mother or my aunt. "He was well muscled. If you told him to do something he didn't want to do, and he had been drinking, you had a fight on your hands."

Twice J.P. was taken to the police station. The cops knew and liked him; he was never booked. My uncle went down once to get him out and another time sent a colleague — all very paternal. My grandfather's drinking bouts were referred to by family members as "toots." But Dodo verbally flayed him for what she considered major transgressions, and his remorse seems to have been genuine, and ineffectual.

A stimulus was the syndicate representatives who came to Memphis to renegotiate the distribution of *Hambone*, which appeared in nearly two hundred newspapers. The syndicate men were Yankees; my grandparents loved setting them up, having them to dinner and then gathering 'round the piano afterward to sing hymns, pretending this was common practice in the South. The Yankees had the last laugh, though: they brought with them good Canadian whiskey, and at some point negotiations would end and serious drinking begin. By the time my grandfather came out of it, the syndicate reps would be back in New York or Chicago, and Dodo would be giving her husband unshirted Arkansan hell.

My grandfather, although never rich, was extremely well paid. The newspaper provided $120 a week; he probably earned as much again from the syndicates. No movie of Hambone emerged, but Jim Alley did put together collections of *Hambone's Meditations* and two volumes of drawings of full-cheeked, proprietary southerners, caricatured in duck blinds and sand traps, called *Distinguished Folks*. They earned him $30,000, an astounding sum at the time. He appeared in *Who's Who* and joined the Tennessee Club and the University Club, where the requirement of a degree was negotiable, and still is.

About this time a person appeared forcefully in their lives who had once been the best-dressed man in St. Louis. He had had a rich bride or two, since disposed of. A president of the United States was said to have attended one of his earlier marriages, in Philadelphia. How this man got to Philadelphia from St. Louis, and what he wore, were never spelled out.

His name was Jack and he sold a variety of things, from

advertising slogans to fancy shotguns. A corpulent but good-looking raconteur with a penchant for hand-cut suits and straw boaters, Jack had wandered most of his life in a haze of privilege, giving up whatever job he had when hunting season began and reporting back to work months later, thicker through the beam from camp dinners cooked by black men in the employ of those planters who enjoyed Jack's deadpan humor and marveled at his wing shooting. He arrived in Memphis as mysteriously as he had arrived in those other cities, presumably at the end of a bird hunt that had taken him through the South, already deaf at a relatively early age and faced with winter in a damp climate.

Jack visited my grandparents and, in the best tradition of southern houseguests, stayed for months. Bridge was the preferred social activity, a game my grandfather was indifferent to and one at which Jack excelled. That Jack and Dodo ended up bridge partners was natural enough. Jack's deafness seems to have added to his appeal; he pretended not to read lips, which provided a conversational advantage to a man already good with words. Communicating with him required notes, minor literary endeavors I engaged in too, much later, that Jack would verbally annotate. In those more social days the scribbling must have been logistically challenging before it became emotionally charged.

There is intimacy in a note, even one between strangers, a connection more basic than the facts it contains. Roles are inherent: mistress and pupil, server and served, loved and lover. Jack would trump this arrangement. The notes Dodo wrote to him were part of the life of a naturally solicitous person but they must have been decisive. I can imagine the two of them exchanging first odd bits of information, then private codas of appreciation, finally admissions of things that may well have been as unavoidable as they were illicit.

4

MEMORY IS a kind of artifact, interpreted in the light of present knowledge and desire. Ascribing motives according to memory, or to the promptings of photographs, letters, and even personal recollections, necessarily involves some presumption. It is so easy to get things wrong, to enhance; and yet to underestimate the force of the past is a worse failing. No amount of speculation can achieve the intensity of the life actually lived.

One photograph in my mother's collection I looked at more than the others. It was taken on the lawn on Highland Avenue in 1931 and shows J. P. Alley sitting on the glider with his two daughters, his golf clubs propped against a table. The awning separates the girls' milky skin from the formidable Memphis sun; their skirts and the sets of their very black hair reflect a shared sense of style. My aunt Elizabeth leans into the camera, legs crossed, a curl on her forehead, more immediately attractive than my mother, Kathryn, a year younger and merely pretty, who sits back and regards the camera coolly.

Not seen are their two brothers, Jimmy and Cal, in the foreground with my grandmother, perhaps swilling lemonade poured from the sweaty pitcher on the table. The brothers' rivalry was real enough but lacked the subtle complexity of their sisters'. Kathryn had recently met, in the presence of Elizabeth, the young man who worked that summer on the loading dock of the ice house down the street — the Conaways knew ice — the most conceited individual she thought she had ever encountered. He was also the most attractive, with a provocative way of raising one eyebrow. Frank Elmer Conaway — "Connie" — had returned from the University of Arizona, without a degree, and had loosely affiliated himself with the Pi Kappa Alpha house in Memphis — a gentleman, when most other boys were, in my mother's opinion, "like wolves."

He asked her out, and she refused — my mother was not to be taken for granted — and so he asked out Elizabeth. Even if my mother had not been interested in him, she wouldn't have viewed this with equanimity. Her relationship with her sister could not be described as simply competitive; the ultimate object of their contention was their father — alternately warm and remote, funny and sad, judicious and intoxicated, laboring in the studio and off on a toot. When J. P. Alley was not their primary focus, other men were substituted; now my mother let Connie know that Elizabeth had recently confused the dates she had made with *two* other suitors, effectively thwarting any romance.

Connie and Kathryn began to see each other in groups of young people and to pair up, casually at first, then determinedly. She was impressed with Connie's dancing, his golf and tennis games, his self-assurance and the trouble he took to make her notice it. When, in someone's kitchen, out of their comrades' hearing, he asked, "Has it ever occurred to you that I might be crazy about you?" she replied truthfully, "Well, yes, in fact, it has."

*

He called her Tassey, I don't know why. They first kissed in a rowboat. When Kathryn boarded the train to Knoxville in September, bound for the University of Tennessee as a sophomore, all the reserve she had brought to her initial meeting with Connie had evaporated, replaced by desperate affection. Their tentative engagement didn't help alleviate this. When the porter brought her a telegram from Connie, the train trundling eastward, she sat in the Pullman saying Connie's words over and over to herself. She was unable to control the urge to communicate with him, right then, despite the fact she had no writing paper. She scribbled a message — on a paper cup.

It was sent, along with a letter on proper stationery, soon after she arrived in Knoxville: "My Connie — I love you. I've already missed you enough to make up for the three months . . . Connie, my own, I worship you so. You are my whole existence — my all — and I'm a tiny bit scared — I feel so very far away from you, Darling, I'm all yours, always, so please take care of us."

Alone, my mother was subject to doubts that she could cope, that people nearby would recognize her and her family's worth, that people elsewhere would remember her. These things reverberated through a correspondence with Connie, in a smooth, slightly ornate hand, her pen a fount of mea culpas maximas, admonitions, and other vague but profound anxieties. Now nothing — sorority life, boys from Nashville and Chattanooga, studies — could distract her. "I get choked," she wrote to Connie the following day. "Yes, I'm crying — and even that doesn't help much — instead of letting some of the misery out, it seems to outrage the desolate feeling I have and I nearly go crazy . . ."

She sent him a telegram expressing her love but knew "those tiny, cold, machine-made letters" wouldn't convey the extremity of her feeling. "I love you — I love you — I love you — I love you." She wrote herself into, and out of, temporary bliss. "Now I feel better and can laugh . . . I honestly believe we'll both die when we're fairly young because we're both entirely too capable of intense feeling to live long — but just think — we'll be about five times as happy as most people are while we're living! . . . I see your eyes telling me you love me — and I'm miserable again."

Coming across these passages half a century later, I experience as much apprehension as insight. The discomfort derives from reconstructing someone else's life through words passionately, privately addressed to another. When those words are my mother's, the feeling I have is of unearned power over a version of her that preceded me, and a painful recognition of themes that would last her lifetime. This exceeds the most compelling argument for truth-seeking on my part. My mother would not have kept and passed along all those love letters if she hadn't valued the contents, but most remain unread by me.

Connie's responses dealt not with her explicit fears or the possibility of an early death, but with the future and his present need, during the Depression, of a job. Yet he is no less caring. "I love you, Dear, as I thought it impossible for me to love any human being." And, "I love you, Kid . . . The future holds so much for us." He isn't averse to yearning, just to my mother's brand of literary anguish. He works endearingly at introspection: "There is no moon tonight, but the stars are out . . . They make a fellow in love think lots of beautiful, if possibly foolish, things. Good for the stars."

Living at home, with no college degree and no clear path into the matrimonial beyond, he depended upon big brother Edwin. They had "conferences." I can see them sitting together as junior and senior executive, carving up the future, Edwin already financially ruined and his grip on any kind of recovery tenuous. They decided that Connie should peddle window-washing equipment to uptown department stores, an unhappy venture. At night, Dad played poker at the ΠΚΑ house.

In Knoxville, Kathryn received a letter from her father addressed to "My own baby." Her favorite course at the time, "advanced art," dealt almost entirely with home furnishings and was indirectly a tribute to J. P. Alley. He wrote soothingly, "I understand that you are in dire distress, which in a member of my family has nearly always meant 'money' . . . I have about come to the conclusion that you are such a fine, sweet and worthwhile little girl, that I am not going to let Connie have you, but keep you for myself just to have around handy when the cream sours, or I fall down the back steps."

Elizabeth meanwhile was leading a carefree, comparatively glamorous life in Memphis, dating the managing editor of the *Commercial Appeal*, an older man with a real job. The two sisters usually dealt with each other drolly, echoes of their father's voice, but Elizabeth was better at it, my mother being too earnest. The year before she had written to Elizabeth, "I can't wash my hair because I haven't any kale to get it waved . . . Tell Mother to make that green organdy into a . . . dress for our dance next Saturday . . . and cut a little flared skirt and fit it on you and have it right at your knee . . ." Now all she wrote about was Connie.

This annoyed Elizabeth. "Dear Ole Soak," she wrote Kathryn in November. ". . . I have for some slow uncertain weeks now been on the very verge of most unreasonably losing my heart to the cutest, most fascinating and adorable little dude that ever pranced around in a derby and a cane. You knew all that, of course, but what you did not know was that I just as suddenly looked him over from a distance one night as he stepped the light fantastic out at The Slipper . . . I could suddenly see myself with an altogether too attractive little husband wagged around for the rest of my life under my left arm while I fed him cocktails with the right. So, darling, your present love affair is still in the lead for pulling in all the flattering attention," but only temporarily.

Elizabeth's "dude" came from Wisconsin — an exotic. He was also named Frank, an uncommon handle and quite a coincidence; now there were two Franks on the Alley horizon. Any similarity between my father and my future uncle ended there, if you discount the glad consumption of whiskey. Elizabeth's Frank would go on to be editor of the *Commercial Appeal* and a power in the city, insistent upon standards in society as well as in bourbon. Six months after Elizabeth wrote that letter he married her, with some spectacle, and took her off to Cuba. He sent his new sister-in-law, Kathryn, a postcard that must have saddened her: "Regards to you and F. Elmer [Conaway]. It's a great life and Cuba is a swell place to make your headquarters while honeymooning."

She was still making her headquarters at 491 South Highland, having dropped out of UT. My father was studying mechanical engineering at Mississippi A & M and living in the ΠKA house. His choice of profession was honorable, their future together uncertain.

My parents were finally married in 1933, with Dad still degreeless and the Depression in full swing. There was no honeymoon in Cuba. They spent some of the next year living in J. P. Alley's studio, and my grandfather typed out a tender document allowing them to stay there "for a period beginning Jan. 1, 1934 and ending the first time J.P.A. has strength enough to whip F.E.C. without outside assistance . . . Rent at the rate of unlimited love and affection payable constantly."

He had discovered that he had Hodgkin's disease, after traveling to Johns Hopkins in Baltimore for diagnosis. Alcohol and cigarettes could not have left him in good physical condition, but he maintained hope that he could overcome a still mysterious, painful malady. He was only forty-eight. Now there was not a political cartoon in the *Commercial Appeal* every day, sometimes not one a week. Hambone was often drawn by his son, Jimmy, the oldest, named for his father but built like a football lineman, which he had been. I think of Uncle Jimmy as the typical son of the famous father, a presumptive hell raiser with an expectation of slight that would be apparent to me even as a small child. One of Jimmy's debauches took him to West Memphis, where, after a fight, he ended up in a hedge, without his shirt, to be extricated by the sheriff and deposited in jail. A phone call from J. P. Alley got him out again and redeposited on the porch at 491 South Highland. My grandfather found him sleeping it off the next morning, pretended that there was nothing extraordinary in the sight of his son's scratched and battered torso flung across the swing, and sent him back to West Memphis with money for the fine.

Kathryn or Elizabeth ministered to their father. Jack, once the best-dressed man in St. Louis, the deaf raconteur, was still in the house, supposedly advising the family about life insurance; I imagine my grandmother drinking iced tea in the kitchen with this itinerant quail shooter who was attaining a status too horrible for anyone to formally recognize. The camaraderie once existing between him and my grandfather had solidified into a grim wait. J. P. Alley confided to my father, on the subject of Jack, "That son of a bitch will get everything."

I have often wondered why he allowed Jack to remain. Politeness counted for a lot: if you were a man, you did nothing and said nothing that might cause offense, unless you were drunk, and then it didn't matter. The rare combination of impoliteness and sobriety could be fatal. But when my grandfather was drunk, why didn't he insult Jack, or shoot him? I think his life had become complicated by fame he didn't know what to do with, and by a rival. I think he saw Jack first as a friend and then as someone who would be in place for Dodo, if Hodgkin's proved stronger than the Alley constitution. It is probable that he never thought about Jack much one way or the other, until the end.

My grandfather died in April, in misery, and was buried in the family plot at Memorial Cemetery. The lead editorial in the *Commercial Appeal* contained, in the midst of a flood of bromides about a full and contented life, some truth. "Fame came to him, but he did not recognize it: he did not understand why persons from afar sought the honor of his acquaintance . . . He was 'one of the boys'. He had a keen mind, [and] an irrepressible sense of humor."

My father decided to return to Arizona, in part, perhaps, to escape the aftermath, knowing my mother needed some relief, and because he liked the place. He and Tassey rode west in a used convertible, leaving their dog to be shipped out later by rail. The oil paintings my mother did of cacti and parched mountains reveal both talent and some tranquility. They lived in a house in the desert near Tucson, rent free, in return for some upkeep, surrounded by saguaro and ocotillo, red rock and the crystalline Catalina Mountains. My father used the ΠΚΑ house in Tucson as a mailing address — he was *the* superannuated frat boy — while the Conaway "ranch" became the hangout for younger collegiates. They smoked Chesterfields sent by my grandmother, who preferred another brand but collected Chesterfield coupons and so sent off the cigarettes by the shoeboxful.

The old snapshots show my mother parting her hair in the middle now, and exposing her face to the Arizona sun. Her smiles lack the theatricality of self-conscious southern belles: no eyelash curlers here, no sister to worry about, and the memory of her father her own. Her younger brother, Cal, came out to visit: skinny, high-strung, a ringer for J. P. Alley. Cal was also a cartoonist, brought along artistically by his father, as Jimmy had been. Shortly before J.P. died he had chosen between his sons, laying hands stained with India ink on Cal, his youngest, rather than on Jimmy; Cal would wear the mantle of political cartoonist at the *Commercial Appeal* while Jimmy became a tire salesman on the back roads of Texas.

Dad, Mom, and Cal rode horses belonging to a real rancher, who hired Connie to help with roundup. Being a bona fide cowboy held more allure than pumping gas in Tucson, which he did at night; Dad bought a pair of spurs with rabbit fur on the straps, and what looks like a ten-gallon hat. The three of them then toured the West; where the money came from I don't know. Connie and Cal, rangy, suntanned, bought western shirts with their names stitched above the pockets, two movie-style wranglers with a comely female companion in white jodhpurs. In Colorado, they were mistaken for rodeo champions, a mistake they did nothing to rectify. Photographs of their visit to Pikes Peak show my parents as hopeful explorers on their own Darien, both knee-deep in leather, safe on the far side of the Continental Divide.

They crossed the Mississippi River, west to east, in late August 1935, the same year Dodo and Jack were married. The older couple went off to St. Petersburg, warmer than Memphis in winter, and spent the following summer in Bucks County, Pennsylvania, much cooler than Memphis; my mother never forgave Dodo and Jack their precipitous behavior or the migratory routine they kept up until the money was gone. Over the years Jack's three-piece suits would disappear, then the gold watch and chain, and the Parker side-by-side shotgun. He kept his amiable defiance, however, and continued to smoke cheap cigars that replaced the dark Havanas that must have once come naturally to the best-dressed man in St. Louis. Their absences did provide an opportunity for my parents, who moved into the house on Highland. Elizabeth was living elsewhere with her Frank, and Tassey's brothers were grown and mostly gone. She and Connie paid some rent and maintained the property, never suspecting that this casual arrangement might evolve into a life.

When grown, I came across a brittle newspaper clipping in a box of family memorabilia that quoted my grandfather on the relevance and immortality of his creation, Hambone. J. P. Alley hadn't put the vernacular into Hambone's mouth to ridicule black people, he said, but to show their essential humanity. I believe that, but I also think he took some advantage of their historical misfortune, and that Hambone outlived my grandfather by too many years.

Bits of J. P. Alley's life still surface: the sign in a souvenir shop in San Antonio on which Hambone rides in a biplane, praising a defunct brand of cigar — my grandfather was casual with copyright — and a book about Memphis found by chance on a library shelf that refers to his "financial troubles," known from Memphis to Mobile, but lost to me. The only enduring lightness shows up in his drawings, his style still deft and unmistakable.

5

THE DESTRUCTION of the Pacific fleet at Pearl Harbor in December 1941 startled and outraged my father. Like most people, he had little idea of where the attack had taken place, or why, but considered the loss of nineteen ships and more than two thousand men a personal affront. His notions of honor and manhood were tested by the sight of younger men joining the Army and steaming out of town to deal with dissembling, murderous foreigners; he, too, was tempted to take off for possible, unspecified glory.

Life for an undegreed mechanical engineer was tolerable. White Memphis in those days was oddly classless, without great disparities in incomes; living was cheap. At home, my parents listened to Bob Hope, Fibber McGee, and *District Attorney* on the radio and slept late on weekends. Dad worked for the American Radiator & Standard Sanitary Corporation, on Beale Street, making a decent salary of three thousand dollars a year, but he was still waiting for a revival of his brother's, and therefore his own, fortune. The appearance of his second child — me — that April had been a disappointment. He and Tassey had a romantic view of the sexually balanced family that my birth disrupted; a girl would also have conspicuously differentiated Tassey from her sister, Elizabeth, who already had two boys and so had been "first" in that particular contest.

Past thirty, my father was professionally and, in some ways, personally inchoate. Both he and my mother had suffered a kind of disinheriting at an early age, Dad through the dissolving of his brother's ice empire, Mom through the death of her father, at the height of his career. It would take a war to unsettle and reassemble them both as the man and woman I came to know.

An army bore some resemblance to a fraternity, where men were men but also boys, unhampered by the niceties of social discourse and free to misbehave in various ways as long as the job got done. Dad never spoke of it this way, and I am speculating when I say this was part of the allure of enlistment. I do know that a year after Pearl Harbor he decided that World War II was a historic phenomenon that demanded his presence, superseding domestic duties and my mother's protests. He had a talent — a basic knowledge of building — that his government needed, and applied for a commission in the Navy's Construction Battalion, the Seabees, to do less than glamorous service putting hammer to nail.

He was disqualified. Although apparently healthy, Dad was color-blind and weighed twenty-four pounds less than the average five-foot-nine American male. A year later he applied again, probably concealing his optical problem, and was accepted by the Navy. Frank Elmer Conaway was made a junior-grade lieutenant by virtue of age and college training and assigned to Camp Peary, the Seabees' training camp near Williamsburg, Virginia.

He left Memphis in the spring of 1943 feeling anything but liberated; when his eastward-bound train crossed Highland

Avenue, he looked up the street toward our house. "The tears started and when I got a last look at Frank's school I was in a hell of a fix," he wrote to my mother. He went to bed and woke up feeling better. True combatants, a colonel and a warrant officer who had been "over" — the euphemism for fighting in Europe — passed the time with him. They were joined by two Royal Air Force pilots on their way back to England, "and we all listened from then on."

At Camp Peary he rose at 5:30 A.M. and took the occasional thirty-mile hike. "There isn't a muscle in my body that isn't sore," he wrote on official Navy stationery emblazoned with crossed anchors and militant bee in sailor's cap, holding wrench, hammer, and machine gun. "If you could see me eat a meal you would think you were with somebody else."

My mother's letters are lively and full of detail; she dutifully set aside her fears in an effort to support and entertain Connie, but sometimes the voice of the former Kathryn Alley gets through. "I'm just going to say it! I miss you. I'm just sick with missing you — I feel dull and bored and blue and listless and I want Connie . . . I knew I'd be bored with you if you . . . didn't get in the swim," but as a consequence, "I'm sunk. I'm mean with the children and I fuss at everybody and I have the jitters all the time."

Many of the Seabees were Dad's age, with wives and children of their own. Dad pointed this out. "War is tough, and women bear the brunt of it but just remember that you are . . . one among millions." His pledges of affection alternated with instructions for paying household bills and the premiums on piddling insurance policies that became a lifelong obsession. He inadvertently exposed my mother's lack of practical knowledge — southern girls took pride in this — and the scantiness of Conaway funds. Meanwhile he progressed from aging, homesick recruit to suntanned officer. He wrote in August. "We have started on the newest and hardest

Commando Run at the station & we have to go over it four times a week & the men once every two weeks. What do you think of that?"

A month into training and already one hundred "boots" were gone, "not being able to stand the gaff" and the rigors of training. Dad is clearly proud of standing both. "It is hard but it is better for their physical defects to come out here than after they leave the country . . . We are having our first inspection this afternoon which will be followed by a . . . competition drill. Think of that, in a month they are to go through, at last, all the motions of seasoned troops."

He was made second in command of the 123rd Battalion, then officer in charge. "How do you like them apples? I'll be the first Lt. (jg) to ever have the job & there have been very few senior Lts. that have had it." He celebrated at the Officers' Club. "I treated myself to a good drunk & boy do I feel better for it! It cleared my head & set me right for another fling at my various duties."

The 123rd was shipped to Camp Endicott, Rhode Island, in September, for penultimate ceremonies before leave. "This thing of battalion organization is no joke . . . Our battalion is to parade in dress blues . . . At the end of the ceremony we will be presented our colors & be commissioned as a battalion ready to do its job." Then the train to Memphis, for leave. "I love you with all my heart and can think or dream of nothing except getting home."

In the final months of 1943 Dad was stationed at Camp Parks, in northern California, where he spent Christmas. "Hold me tight in your heart tonight & dream of the time to come," he wrote, "when you will again hold me tight in your arms & make me feel safe from all the troubles & free from all the fears that feed upon me when I am separated from you. This has not been a Merry Xmas."

A similar note is sounded by my mother. "Connie — I love you so — don't let this separation take us away from each other — your life is so strange to me now — and you have so many interests and I have less than ever because of being so tied down and weighted down with everything."

Her letters, undated, the envelopes lost, make up an emotional continuum held together by those dashes, full of love, encouragement, complaints about lack of stylish clothes and proper distractions, self-pity, and outright loss of control. When I, not yet three, climbed a ladder left against the house by workmen and crawled to the peak of the roof, Mom enticed me down and then beat me with a dog leash, raising welts that persisted for days. She presented this to my father as an example of what she had to put up with — invasions of adult equanimity, never-ending domestic Pearl Harbors. "He is absolutely the most unpredictable child I ever saw. *Nothing* daunts Jim. He is going to do that which he thinks of doing, come what may. And he *thinks* of the most unthinkable things."

"I know how tough it is for you," Dad wrote in early January, ". . . Keep your chin up my Angel & I'll be home to take that same adorable chin in my hands and kiss you as soon as I can."

Always there were bills — from Oak Hall, where our clothes were bought, from the utilities, from a doctor my mother was consulting for a mysterious ailment. My father advised her to sell a war bond, a near-worthless lot in midtown he had inherited, and, if necessary, the car. His big brother, Edwin, had moved from Memphis to Dallas and had problems of his own. "I have had but one letter from Edwin since I've been in Calif. which I answered . . . & again asked him for money." Dad got only a bottle of hand lotion from his brother. "That is the ending of the reading of that lesson," and a watershed, since he had realized at last that Edwin could not provide for him.

He was broke but freighted with gifts from his men working in the shops: name placards, knives, a file cabinet, foot locker, canvas duffels, rings made out of welding rods, gadgets. "It's a lot of fun," he wrote, "but what do you do with all this stuff?" His men were "the toughest, roughest bunch of cookies you ever saw and there is nothing they are not . . . willing to kick the hell out of at the drop of a hat." That included soldiers encountered in San Francisco.

The romance of the city in wartime was apparently lost on Dad, who spent a fair amount of his time getting his men out of jail and taking heat from his superiors for their behavior. He tacitly approved of beating up soldiers. "I raise hell with them, restrict their liberty, assign them to long night jobs or duty ones, take them off the boxing team. They get large fines or days in the brig on bread and water," and still he heard approving statements about himself: "'The Co B.–C.O. (Commanding Officer) will pop your ass but he is a right guy.'"

Preparations were made for Mom to visit that involved a transcontinental train trip. "Each day that passes now I get happier," Dad wrote in early February 1944. ". . . You are really coming to me. I love you so much."

He shipped out right after the visit, first to "Pearl," then Midway, which had been taken by Admiral Nimitz two years before, in the first defeat of the Japanese, and turned into a staging area. Homesick, heavily dependent upon the mail flights, he worked hard to fill the time, and played tennis and dived for cat's-eyes on the reef. "I guess this is one of the few places on earth where it is necessary to wear sun glasses even though it is raining." Navy censors didn't permit him to mention Midway. "You make life wonderful & complete . . . When this mess is over & done with I have a wife whom I idolize & who loves me completely to go home to."

My mother addressed him as "Lavender Ears" in one letter, a reference to sunburn, and lovingly accused him of being a playboy. In another, she told of enrolling in art school and of her determination, should the lot be sold, to spend the money. "I know you won't approve and Mother would have a double-jointed fit, if she knew I planned to — but I'm going to. My nerves are still in deplorable shape" — what I think was the effect of loneliness and an inability to believe in her own, isolated worth. "I get uncontrollable fits of shaking and throbbing and get frightened and can't stop it — and the only release is to get fervently interested in something . . . I may spend a little money on the house, and a little money on some clothes — and have a little fun. Forgive me — but our future happiness depends on it."

Soon she was soothing Dad again, her talk of distractions forgotten. "Don't be blue and discouraged, darling. This will all be over one of these days and we'll all be together again, and be happy again — and I, for one, will have had my values straightened out . . . so that I'll be capable of making my three boys a lot happier. Gone are the days of wishing for a lot of senseless things."

A construction mishap left my father with a broken rib and a hernia, so he couldn't participate in the athletic contests (including a "boxing free for all") marking the first anniversary of the formation of the 123rd Battalion. He was operated on for the hernia and spent two months recuperating. Then he was unexpectedly transferred to Peleliu. The main fighting there had taken place while Dad was in the hospital; it was some of the most harrowing of the war. Ten thousand Japanese soldiers had to be pried out of coral bunkers; the name Bloody Nose Ridge became a Marine badge of honor.

For my father, Peleliu was a graduation of sorts. The island's caves still contained some of the enemy when he arrived; Tokyo may have known the war was lost, but not those Japanese soldiers in hiding. There were skirmishes in the mountains, and a bloated enemy officer was found floating in a jungle pool. Dad spent as much time with Marines as with fellow Seabees, living in a tent and shaving out of his helmet. Japanese planes dropped bombs on the runway, and he supervised the filling of the holes so the American planes could take off and blow holes in the enemy's runways. "The sight and smell of the dead is a horrible thing but that too you get somewhat accustomed to."

I believe that this was as close to a beach assault as my father got. He spent another Christmas away from home, blue but resigned. A letter from a discharged Seabee must have touched him. "Do you know Mr. Conaway now that I am out of the outfit and look back to the days I was always gitting [*sic*] into trouble I never knew what a good Joe you were all so fair to the men under your command." The end of the war lay eight months in the future; I don't know how Dad spent them, and the Navy is no help. The letters between Dad and home were not saved. The last of the fighting in the Pacific, including the dropping of the atomic bombs in the summer of 1945, goes unrecorded.

Early that same year, my mother decided to have an operation for the internal complication that had bothered her for years, the first of several elective surgeries she would undergo periodically. Neither she nor Dad ever wrote or spoke of this one in terms other than the symptoms the operation was supposed to correct: headaches, weakness, distraction, panic. Whatever the malady, it provided the stimulus for her recurring, epic despair. Her mother's trips to St. Petersburg and Bucks County left Tassey feeling doubly deserted; when Dodo was home, the presence of Jack reminded my mother of her father and his unappeasable death.

Surgery for the mysterious ailment was done. In March my grandmother wrote to Dad, somewhere in the Pacific. "Kathryn is in good condition . . . But she was in such a nervous state and had borne up too long before she ever gave up to have this done, so that her reaction now is just about that of a complete nervous breakdown . . . I am just trying to tell you how things are and not to worry about it because she is getting herself a little better in hand each day . . . I wish I had 'raised my daughter to be a soldier' — and in a way of course she *has* been one, but still demands a little something special in every situation. The boys are all right. Jimbo may not miss his mother more than Frank does but he says more about it . . . Frank says nothing but I am sure *feels* a lot deep in his own heart.

"Memphis is beautiful with Spring, as you remember."

6

HERE IS what I remember of the war: jumping on empty tin cans, mashing them flat, so they could be sent off to be made into "bullets." A hailstorm that tore screens from the house. My mother singing the song

Mares eat oats,
And does eat oats,
And little lambs eat ivy.
A kid'll eat ivy, too,
Wouldn't you?

Here is what I learned, years later: Mom went to New Orleans to recover from the stress of the operation and while there consulted a psychiatrist, a radical procedure that could not be undertaken in Memphis, where someone might find out. She stayed in the French Quarter and took art instruction, a convenient excuse for being away, as well as an opportunity to indulge her passion. Presumably my grandmother paid for all this but not, I'm fairly sure, for what followed: visits to the doctors, pills, varying degrees of "help" in the form of black women who came sporadically to the house. My mother's insistence that she was unequal to life's physical demands may have reflected a remnant view of "ladies" as frail things; it prefigured a life where the concern with illness greatly outstripped the actual incidence of it. The possibility of getting sick, like the suspicion that sickness lay in wait, provided an excuse, often unwitting, for not doing things that might have led her — us — out of a preoccupation with other pitfalls. My mother's emotional and physical strength, as Dodo had suggested, was there, though disguised and always complicated, and would be revealed, in time, in the most unlikely circumstances.

I was stuttering when Mom got back from New Orleans. We had been looked after by an old Arkansas friend of Dodo's, a squat, chain-smoking harridan whom I wiped from memory and who filled me, when she visited us, with inexplicable loathing. The day the war ended, people blew their car horns, not normally allowed in Memphis and therefore riveting. I expected Dad to be home the next day but he didn't arrive for months. Then this man was living with us who did something called shaving and carried with him the medicinal smell of white cream from a blue jar. He said funny things sailors were supposed to say, like "Now hear this" and "Do as I say and not as I do." He mowed the grass and built a fence.

Soon Mom was writing to Dodo, in St. Petersburg, "I can't get any kind of help I can depend on with the children . . . Doing the purely mechanical things of keeping house leaves my mind free to worry over the whole mess." The whole mess included what she saw as an inability to recover from the operation and her breakdown, a lack of funds, my father's discontent in his role of furnace salesman. "If I could only have some time to read, even, and go out to see people and have people in — I think, in time, I might be able to get myself straightened out . . . If I could get some hope in my heart for the future . . . I need gaiety — and enthusiasm — and I need it over a period of time."

Any thought of the past or future "racks my body and head with such pain it is unbearable. It's not a case of feeling sorry for myself, Mother — it's a case of dying of heartache." Even reading *Peter Rabbit* to "poor little lost Jim" reminded her of toil and separation from an imaginary, brighter life. "Do you see, Mother, why I say I need you? . . . If Jack doesn't want to come back — let him stay down there for awhile . . . Jack makes you resent having to lift an eyelash."

My parents had planned a second honeymoon but there was no money for that or for a down payment on their own house. This might have been financed by the government, an arrangement available to vets, but Dad was either unable to raise cash or, more likely, uninterested in shouldering a mortgage. He was either disillusioned with the America he had returned to, or caught up in old problems that years and distance had not solved, or both. His and my mother's discontent seems even sadder when I consider the ardor of their letters to each other while he was in the Pacific, and their transcendent expectations. These would never die, and they set up a different sort of tension, one between present and future that proved unresolvable. We were all left, I think, with a romantic notion of success — of happiness — as something always just beyond our grasp, requiring more than ambition, hard work, and, ironically, the observance of Memphis's conventions that my parents so valued.

The house on Highland had only three bedrooms and a broad attic, part of the stolid immutability of middling white Memphis. The hallway under the throbbing industrial fan doubled as an alley for clamorous ball games between my brother Frank and me. Three generations contended for access to a single bathroom. An enclosed back porch served as a breakfast nook until my father "modernized" the kitchen by building a bar and adding stools. My brother and I perched to supervise the frying of bacon and, if we were lucky, the washing of dishes by a dark figure in a white apron who snorted at our silliness.

The chimney in the living room led to outer space; the fireplace smelled of ruin. The dining room contained a big table, a sideboard, and a glass cabinet for Dad's family's imponderables — ancient pickle forks, etched goblets, elves' utensils (salt dispensers). One window overlooked the driveway, a big oak, and the street that led north toward Central Avenue and forever.

My parents' bedroom, beyond the dark rectangular frame at the foot of the stairs, contained two windows and, between them, a mirror where my mother sits, tiny brush in hand, containers open on the vanity. She combs out dark, lustrous hair, head canted, as intent upon the reflected spectacle as I. This is linked in my mind to a certain red dress and the manner Mom assumed when she wore it: poised, regal, destined for some social greatness hovering indistinctly in both our minds. A man — my father, or hers — once said that Tassey was the most beautiful woman he had ever seen descend a staircase. Unfortunately ours led only to the attic and so a woman in a red party dress would have no reason to be coming down it. I wondered where that other staircase was, and who had stood at the bottom. I had the impression that the special occasion in her past would be repeated, that dressing table and staircase leading nowhere would be replaced by a sweeping balustrade and a large, ornate room from which drifted the sound of singing.

Mom and Dad would leave the house relaxed, offhand, happy. But when they were not going out, a net went over Mom's hair, "angel wings" were spread over her forehead to suppress wrinkles, and dank, woeful creams took the place of lipstick and perfume. Then I felt something else entirely. This was capitulation to the demands of the present, to awful limits. The creams I associated with the pills in "Mommy's" life, nothing drastic, just a dwindling trail of pharmacological steppingstones leading into a version of the future utterly at odds with the first one. She was no invalid but she talked a lot about being sick; my recognition that some of these maladies weren't real made me feel guilty, dreading discussions of symptoms and at the same time abnormally aware of them.

I wanted to be in their bedroom when I was sick. Then adults put their heads through the doorway and sized me up with proper concern; the blankets smelled pathetically of convalescence — autumnal wool, mothballs — and the radio murmured, convenient at my right hand. Kitchen sounds came from a place more distant than the Yukon, more penumbral than the Shadow's haunt; chicken soup arrived on a wooden tray with treacherous folding legs, Mom's sweetly smiling face above it.

Supper in the dining room involved the residual conflict between grand expectations and limited means. A bell summoned the maid, when there was a maid to summon. It didn't always work as it should, and even when it did work the maid was slow to come and unenthusiastic about holding a dish of turnip greens or mashed potatoes for us to dip into. Glacially, eonically, she would progress around the table toward me, pausing in thought, captivated by something in a landscape that included, as far as I could tell, only the façade of St. Luke's Methodist Church across the street. My mother's exasperation was no match for this collective, historical reverie.

The diners included my parents, my brother — blond, crew-cut, worldly — that older man named Jack who was my grandmother's husband but *not* my grandfather, a crucial distinction, and Dodo. Her ample nose and black eyes amidst the crow's-feet I associated with an Indian ancestor, a delicate subject in our family concerned with what was known in

Memphis as lineage. My mother and my aunt Elizabeth insisted that we were descended from a Cherokee princess "from the very best Cherokee family." They disapproved of the sack dresses Dodo wore around our house in hot weather, when she wasn't summering in Bucks County, because they were country.

Dodo smoked strong cigarettes and made cornbread in an iron skillet. Her Jack was in the family but not *of* it, and he couldn't hear. Adults were forever scribbling on a pad he carried in his shirt pocket. I felt sorry for Jack, being left out of things, even as I recognized my mother's detestation of him. He spent most of his time in a rocker on the porch, reading Zane Grey novels and smoking Tampa Nuggets. I can see his bay window and steely hair like a riverboat gambler's, his bare legs beneath trousers hiked up to get the breeze, his nudging of the rocker into barely perceptible motion. Cinders from his cigar went down the back of my pajamas one Christmas morning, the only harm he ever did me, and that inadvertent. Yet I resented his exemption from the drudgery of washing dishes, a task done by all when a maid didn't do it for us. Once a year, shamed into helping, Jack would pick up a towel and a wet plate, and broken crockery would litter the linoleum. Jack would swear elaborately, complaining in his singsong, deaf man's voice of Yankee winters that had crippled his hands just as they had ruined his hearing. Those same hands would soon be lighting up a cigar and cracking pulp fiction.

Jack once told my mother, when she claimed kinship with President Buchanan, "You're the only person I know proud to be descended from a bachelor."

The enmity went deeper; I accepted it as one of life's mysterious givens. When my father perniciously suggested that Jack wasn't deaf at all, that he had faked it to get out of working, I stood behind Jack's rocker and screamed. He didn't flinch. When I crawled underneath and took the change that spilled from his pockets, Jack took no notice. When I threw a hunting knife that pierced the screen in his bedroom and came to a quivering halt two feet from him, that leonine head simply turned and dipped in recognition of the fact that, indeed, a knife was stuck in the window frame. Then he went back to reading.

Attached to the garage was a shack referred to grandiosely as the servants' quarters. My brother and I stand inside, in the corner behind the door, barefoot in shadows redolent of ashes and sweat, and watch a black man chase a black woman around the iron frame bed. She is our maid and she wears only a slip, and cuts at the man with a razor strop. Stripped to the waist, his torso a lustrous, light-collapsing ebony, he takes the blows on that smooth twilight topography of muscle and tendon, then comes to us in the corner and says in mock rage, "Look'a dare."

This is innocent theater, but illicit and so terribly exciting. Across the man's forearm lies a white welt. There is no blood, and I am convinced he has nothing in common with my own blanched, insignificant origins. I watch as he catches the woman and tumbles her, squealing with laughter, onto the soiled ticking, turns her over his knee, and with an open palm spanks one mound of soft brown flesh and then the other.

I don't remember their names. She was one in the procession of women who strolled up our driveway, past the fire of daffodils in the hedgerow between our house and the Brinkmans'. Her lover cut grass in the neighborhood when he wasn't boxing. My father liked him — he didn't know what Frank and I witnessed — and took him with us to the gravel pit south of town to shoot the .22 pistol.

I wondered why this man was called a yard boy. He disappeared, and some years later returned. I saw him standing on the other side of Highland Avenue, staring at our house, and went over to talk to him. He had become, he told me, a middleweight contender. That didn't mean much to me, but I had been with my father and brother while they listened to a radio broadcast of one of his matches; I realized that life is unpredictable, and I will never forget the sight of his beautiful alligator shoes.

Many families we knew had help of some sort, even families with little money. The Conaways' was part-time, an arrangement that often foundered on my mother's complicated demands, if not on a lack of ready cash. Maids were paid eight dollars a week during the war, then fourteen, then twenty. Their names echo back along the constricting tunnel of memory: Bea, Dolly, Mary, Carrie. I thought of them as people hired to *not* do what my mother expected, or to do it with immense deliberation. Mom complained that they were untrained; I imagined a school somewhere that prepared black women to more efficiently bring me a glass of milk, to cook black-eyed peas with fatback, to iron cotton dresses that went limp in the humidity. I think that having a maid was as important as getting the work done, a link to the old, largely fanciful aristocratic South.

I understood that maids weren't "equal" before I recognized separate drinking fountains and segregated bathrooms. I saw their faces in the rear windows of passing buses after they had shed their aprons at the end of the day and walked down the driveways to stand and wait on curbs, intimate but unreconciled factors there and in the house, on the picked-up edges of our lives. Why was so much — collecting our garbage, hanging our curtains, spreading our mayonnaise — dependent upon them, and why did they consent to do these things? And why would someone put a black man's ears in a jar of alcohol, as I had heard, and put the jar in the window of a barbershop just north of the city line?

*

Above our garage and the dilapidated, finally abandoned maid's room was the loft. Climb rungs nailed to the wall, push up the trap door into baking shadows full of wasps and spears of sunlight, swing the hinged windows open onto infinite, luminous possibility. Those big east Memphis lots, dynastic in breadth and diversity, stitched together in the corners by tangles of honeysuckle, formed a patchwork savanna. Below lay trash burner, woodpile, grape trellis. Fruit collected from it and boiled down in the big aluminum pot by Dodo and my mother was poured into jars, turning them a translucent lavender; they smelled of hot paraffin, sticky-sweet. The tulip poplar beyond the grape trellis was encompassed by a table, Dad's latest project. On the edge of our property stood the diminutive white studio, container of clues into family history and the abiding value of the Alleys, an idea that was never stated, just evoked.

7

THE FAMILY in the house on the south side of ours would have been acceptable to my mother if they hadn't rented their top floor to a fireman and their cottage out back to a divorcée. She wore very red lipstick and her overweight boyfriend drove an old Buick, but worse was the fireman, a lumbering Mississippian who lived with his family above the main house. He had a boy my age, Purnell, who spoke with a twang and ended every question with the imperative "say!" Purnell also said "ain't," and "twiest" instead of "twice," and his mother's "Pur-nehhhhh-*yull!*" issuing several times a day from the serpentine back steps leading up to their doorway made my mother cringe. "They aren't our sort of people," she would tell me. I understood what she meant but wondered exactly who our sort of people were.

Purnell's father worked odd hours and slept a lot. His older brother became a policeman, suspended twice — twiest — for beating people up, but Purnell was sweet-tempered and obliging, as skinny as I and more daring: he jumped from the studio roof into leaf piles and ventured behind the divorcée's house, but I couldn't depend on him. His mother's call would cause his mouth to pucker, his pale eyes to grow large, and eventually his hands to shake before he tore himself away from the most interesting enterprise and ran home.

Next to his house was the doctor's, converted to an office, and behind that a shack occupied by a black family. In the brutal acceleration of childhood memory, that garden becomes a parking lot for the doctor's expanded clientele and the black family shrinks to a solitary old man who smokes a pipe and sits motionless behind his screen door. Then he is gone and the shack razed, and concrete and macadam creep into a view once ruled by grass snakes and dandelions.

Beyond the doctor's stood one more house, on the commercial frontier, bought by the furniture supplier just across the alley and converted to storage, a pathetic sight without inhabitants, new lawn furniture piled on the porch and loungers and sofas wrapped in paper crammed into the rooms. This was the beginning of Normal, the old stop on the Southern Railroad named for the teachers' college built about the time my grandparents arrived and since absorbed by the city, a curtain of storefronts including the ice house where my parents met, a variety store reefed with toys and everything necessary for daily existence, and the Normal Tea Room, where gawky aspiring math and science instructors from Hattiesburg or Jackson ate breaded veal cutlets and drank Dr. Peppers.

In the barbershop, between customers, a sepulchral man slipped behind a curtain to take nips, eliciting from my mother the pained smile of the student of human weakness: whiskey wasn't the barber's fault. Fletcher's Drug Store, smelling of something medicinal, offered milky stone tabletops, chairs with backs of twisted wire, and comics arrayed solely for the pleasure of small boys. Once a day a Negro man in shoes mashed flat in the back sprinkled green grit on the hexagonal white tiles and pushed it with a broad broom out to the pavement. A dime bought a tub of root beer and shaved ice from a shiny-domed sodaman whose patience with his juvenile customers seems in retrospect saintly: he allowed us to imagine ourselves Red Ryder or some other avatar for hours, beneath the lapping blades of the ceiling fan and then in the frigid glory of air conditioning.

On Saturday afternoons in the Normal Theater we watched Roy Rogers and Trigger bow their heads beneath the rose trellis, to pray before storming the citadels of outlawry. This praying turned us into cynics. Cowboys affirmed not so much a need for violence as an ability not to be afraid of it — of being beaten up, humiliated, or deprived and left in some bitter western gloaming beyond the reach of family and friends. We were unforgiving critics. After seeing Gene Autry pursue a bully up a hill, revealing his broad backside in fringed white trousers, I could barely stand him or the sound of his guitar. Randolph Scott was tolerable — he could knock a man down and not worry about what happened next — but easily distracted by women. The best scenes were filled with armed horsemen riding away from the camera and from anything relating to responsibility. Then the lights would come up and the doors swung open and the stale smell of popcorn would be pushed in by air from the hot, overexposed pavement. I would see myself mirrored in the purple front of the jewelry shop, infused with cinematic courage, a protean figure emerging from a submarine grotto.

How strange to be from a place called Normal. More interesting than Normal's façade was what lay behind it, the weed-choked world of parked cars, rear exits, and refuse, busy with the comings and goings of suppliers and carriers-away, scalded cats and mutts on leave from their yards, like us. Purnell and I were forbidden to go "behind the stores," a dark phrase carrying more than the weight of the alleys. But we went anyway, to peruse what Fletcher's had thrown out, not *Red Ryder* but magazines full of doughy-looking women in their underwear and boxers with bloody faces. Behind the grocer's lay fruit in crates that must be thrown, and bottles for breaking. Once we climbed into the back of a truck belonging to a black man and jumped up and down on his collection of discarded cardboard until he caught and swung us to the ground, saying, "This ain't Miss'ippi." We didn't know what that meant, but felt violated.

The low shed at the back of the tea room provided access to the roof. Once up, we proceeded with impunity along the lofty, tarred, connected tops of barbershop, drugstore, hardware, bank. The view was of the working world: gas stations and railroad tracks and the arching sameness of residential streets girding us against a world beyond Normal. The low brick crown of storefronts provided cover for spying on pedestrians and later for dropping water bombs and wielding purloined aerosol cans that projected globs of shaving cream with force and accuracy.

Every now and then the world was constricted by the shriek of the fire siren. A number of things happened at once: Mr. Brinkman, who sold insurance, rushed from the house next door, a cigar in his mouth, rolling as fat men do in a hurry. People appeared on the porches and curbsides of Normal, watching for the appearance of the ladder truck. Dogs became edgy. Everything ceased in expectation of glorious disaster. I would see Purnell's father's large, sleepy face under a black helmet as the engine clamored past; there was no sense of danger, just an irresistible cessation of adult activities and expectations. Only Jack ignored this loud, official anarchy. Then the neighborhood would settle back into its ways and I would feel a loss, as of a promise unfulfilled, the fire being far away and the struggle, too.

We lived for aberrations, the disruption of the norm. Storms were the best, drifting mats of precipitation that flailed at the trees and filled ditches with dark torrents running toward some imagined, uncontrollable flood. One freakish winter, cold wind carrying down the Mississippi depended monstrous icicles from trees and bent them southward. Snow in the streets, that fabulous rarity, meant sledding on the waterworks hill. Far better was being towed behind the family car, on a rope, the runners cutting through the slush to tarmac, grinding around corners with Dad looking back to see that all was well in what amounted to sanctioned daredevilry. The sense of abandon that came down with the snow would deposit my father in the kitchen of a friend, where at noon on a Saturday, wearing his old Navy windbreaker, he and the friend would drink a little bourbon in celebration of the elements, or something. Then he would get back into the car and tow us home again.

Dad taught his sons to shoot pool and to always think about the second shot. The occasional trip to the gravel pit to fire the .22 pistol combined his regard for weapons with some mechanical ingenuity. He constructed from rods and galvanized metal cut-out targets that spun when hit, an elaborate concoction marveled at by the crowd of bare-chested boys out there to blast tin cans and snakes. Dad's advice was classic, soothing: breathe out before you shoot, squeeze the trigger. You shouldn't know when the gun will fire, and if you do, you've rushed it. The spinning metal rabbit involved a wash of pride — his and mine.

School was part of the same geographical designation: three blocks away, through a hedge and across a campus where a cow grazed my first year, the Greek portico of the Normal Training School signaled something both craved and feared. To prepare for it I had to have new clothes from Oak Hall and a sampling of pencils and notepads, a medley of bright colors that served as passport to the status of schoolboy. My mother went with me for the crucial selection of the teacher, which was in fact an assignment, to a building that was part of the teachers' college but separate, an immeasurable journey across open space that smelled of crabgrass baking in the September sun and resounded with bells and kids screaming in a dusty yard clotted with bicycles.

South of the school was the railroad, and beyond it rows of narrow houses and duplexes where people lived who were not our sort, either. "The wrong side of the tracks" carried hard, ready associations for me, since most of the students came from there; many of them said "ain't." The presence of a big brother at Normal Training School was important. Five years older than I, Frank the ferocious, possessor of the mitered blond crew cut, faced down surly older boys and hurled my antagonists into bushes even when I "started" it and then stood, listening to the imaginative exchange of insults.

An older Training alumnus would go on to prison, maybe an inevitability. He brought a revolver to school late one afternoon and fired it in the direction of the geography teacher, Miss Lee, too old to hear the shots or to notice puffs of dust fore and aft as she made her way across the otherwise deserted campus toward the bus turnaround, final stop on the eastward route.

When I turned eight my mother was pregnant again. We spent a day beside the lake in Shelby Forest, north of the city, where she lay in a hammock Dad had strung between trees, the hint of what would become a watermelon under her dress. He cooked the hotdogs while my friends and I pursued frogs; later, he sat with his back against the tree, looking at my mother with a patience that touched me even as it made me wonder.

I didn't adjust well to my brother Dan's birth. When he was a year old I put a toy cricket in his crib that leapt about and terrified him; I hid in the attic above his room and made monster sounds. One afternoon Dad took me for a drive in our green Hudson, with its gracefully striated rotundity and step-down floorboards, and denounced my general behavior. "You can put that in your pipe and smoke it," he repeated. I didn't get the metaphor and for once was innocent of a specific charge: breaking windows in the basement of the furniture store. I blamed myself not just for smashed glass and sibling abuse but for tensions I didn't understand.

In retrospect, my childhood seems extraordinarily free. On summer mornings I was up and out the bedroom window without breakfast — duties lurked behind the Quaker Puffed Rice — wearing shorts and nothing else, to range with impunity. When the equatorial noon caught me I simply went to sleep; once I woke up on grass next to the pavement, under a circle of concerned adult faces, and went about my business only slightly embarrassed. There was nothing to harm me and my friends. Electronic pollution was limited to radio programs, movies, and Milton Berle, the only television show, tedious but to be watched solely for the proximity to the machine. Frank and I had to go to our cousins' for that experience. The imagination was mercifully undirected since the Conaways were one of the last families to get a television set, not sagacity on my parents' part but an effect of our squeezed finances. By then the written word had been established as a route out of boredom and the heat.

The sticky furnace of Highland Avenue in July could be replaced with the interior of the library built next to the Methodist church: marble floors cold beneath bare feet, rungs of chairs that left cool stripes across the bare back, slabs of refrigerated wood that supported elbows and cool, open books. The words Dodo jotted down — funny comments from my brothers and me, adults' droll insights into the unavoidable failings of one another — and later used for *Hambone,* linked her to some broader arena. She substituted these words in the balloons of cartoons drawn now by her sons, and resold to the syndicate. And we all wrote notes to Jack, which were exposed in his singsong renditions; I learned that public humiliation was lessened by a few words well organized.

My cousins' lives seemed glamorous by comparison. My aunt Elizabeth's house, in Chickasaw Gardens, sat amidst mock Tudors and Norman castles, Spanish colonial haciendas and plain outsized American homes shoulder to shoulder in their significance. On Christmas morning we would arrive with our modest gifts and heavy expectations, intruding upon the life of regnant Memphis. I could tell that my mother felt a thrill entering her sister's house; at the same time I sensed her jealousy. Dad remained hale, and out of place. My aunt's living room, half the size of our entire downstairs, impressed me with its windows — floor to ceiling, with diamond-shaped panes and lead mullions. There were more bathrooms than we could use. Various hallways supported reefs of photographs of my aunt and her husband, now editor of the *Commercial Appeal*, at Cotton Carnival and other enviable events. Uncle Frank's bearing attested to his position in the community; his distinctive nasal honk paralyzed me with its directness and far-reaching, barely comprehensible importance.

Not only did Uncle Frank and Aunt Elizabeth — "Sister" — have maids, they also had a butler, a black man and the most reticent human being I had ever encountered, devoted to keeping Uncle Frank away from people who might bother him, including his own sons and nephews. The butler did not prepare food; he delivered it, on trays, after it had been arranged by the cook. He moved in a netherworld between rulers and ruled, in black tie and white jacket that offset his dark, inscrutable face. Once I caught him reading the newspaper in the breakfast room, but usually he hovered between the two realms, close to invisible, impossible to get around.

Our cousins were roughly our ages; they shared their bounty — candy, firecrackers, costumes, wheeled and pointed objects of all sorts, and guns, both playful and, later, real ones. The accumulation at the base of their big, decked-out spruce on the sun porch was half the joy of Christmas. There were wonders Frank and I hadn't even known existed: puzzles, foreign bikes, an air gun designed to shoot a donut of wind across the room. Clearly Santa stopped in Chickasaw Gardens before he got to Highland Avenue. The adults drank toddies, cleared their throats, and gazed between the mullions at the rolling lawn and the brick wall separating it from the district attorney's. Sometimes a short, florid man came over for a drink who wore a vest and made ribald comments that only Uncle Frank seemed to understand. This was the district attorney himself; he drank scotch, not bourbon, and so gave away to the garbagemen the many fifths of Tennessee's best product that naturally found their way onto his desk every year. The word had gotten around. A dozen black men gathered on the street on Christmas morning, hands in pockets, casting sidelong glances up the long driveway.

There was some determining factor beyond money that made my cousins' lives much more appealing than ours, but I couldn't figure out what that was. At times I felt condescended to, but put up with it for the fun available. This made me feel dishonest, and this in turn led to a certain licentiousness, a ready participation in most of the things we were clearly not supposed to do. One day my cousin cocked his air blunderbuss and upended a can of talcum powder into the muzzle. We took cover in a bunker of furniture and waited for the inevitable. "You come outa there," demanded the maid, a broad young woman in a new uniform. My cousin's calm determination, the gun resting on his knees, petrified me. She moved into range, warily, and he pulled the trigger. A white cloud engulfed us. When the particulate had settled I saw revealed a monumental piece of sculpture, a blanched Rushmore with dark slits for eyes, talcum scree crumbling from cheeks and brow. I remember then the sight of my cousin leaping through the house like an ape, inches from this suddenly animated, enraged statue.

The nights I slept over, the butler would allow us access to the master bedroom after our suppers had been eaten, to briefly view its occupants. My aunt and uncle lay there in separate beds, trays set up in front of them for late, luxurious dining, and spread over Uncle Frank's coverlet was a slew of newspapers. Each edition of the *Commercial Appeal* was hand-delivered to him from the printing plant on Union Avenue so he could peruse the headlines and see what deserved page one and what didn't. Often he was on the telephone, directing the city editor to change something, parrying complaints from politicians or preparing a friend for bad news the following morning. He would honk at us, my aunt would utter a few welcoming words, and then we would be ushered back up the corridor and turned out in the big house, to misbehave until we fell unconscious.

8

FOR A WHILE Dad kept an office downtown, in the old Sterick Building off Court Square. My mother and brothers and I would sometimes drive down to pick him up after work, a jaunt that qualified as an adventure if we looped around to Front Street and glimpsed the Mississippi. Dad relished the river and its unsavory associations as something colorful and historically significant, but he rarely got on it. That roiling, caramel-colored plain of water was not to be approached casually, and could be dangerous.

Our outdoor excursions were tamer affairs, usually undertaken with a cumbersome old canoe Dad bought secondhand, an indestructible vessel too heavy for one person to carry and nearly impossible to tip over. We took it to Moon Lake, in Mississippi; to Kentucky Lake, part of a watery world created by the Tennessee Valley Authority and ruled by spoonbill catfish and big motor launches out in the main channel; and once to the Ozarks. We camped, but only after exhaustive searches. My mother required the right composition of trees, sky, and water that contained few country people in ailing pickups and no blacks whatsoever. Cow patties, even brittle ones, could disqualify the most promising site. The right to refuse was important to her. Dad contained his impatience during these rambling assessments — dust settling on the car hood, the sun doing things to the road ahead — because if he didn't, Mom would wash her hands (her phrase) of the whole affair and then the responsibility fell on him.

The search would continue until, exhausted, famished for a swim, we would at last find the right place and tumble to get the tent up and the canoe off the car, to satisfy every military contingency before the water could be approached. Then arguments slipped away in the lubricious suspension of lake or river; my father, spindle-legged, barrel-chested, bobbed on his back, hands behind his head, a natural wonder that caught the attention of other campers and elicited from my mother, sitting in a chair at water's edge, an appreciative smile.

The canoe belonged to a contingent of outmoded gear passed down, in some cases for generations, and still used because new equipment was expensive. Dad sent me off to play football in pads he had used in junior high, bits of cracked leather held together with cord, and a leather helmet. The other boys treated me like a walking museum exhibit, and the organizer of the team forbade me to play because he considered the stuff dangerous. Among my grandfather's leavings was a split bamboo fly rod, a noodly thing put together in sections, with an extra tip kept in a length of cane with a brass screw top. I used the rod the time my parents retrieved me from scout camp and we set up our tent beside the Spring River. No one I knew was interested in fly-fishing, a bizarre pastime in a world of crank baits and frog gigs. In shorts and tennis shoes, I waded up to my armpits in Ozark runoff and lashed the water along the bank; unexpectedly something rose to my fusty fly, a corona of bright silver that miraculously tightened the line, thrashing in nethery weeds.

Old golf clubs — rusty blades in rotten canvas bags — lay about the house, and tennis rackets warped into huge mesh spoons. Also the expensive double-barreled shotgun of Jack's, and a single that had been my grandfather's. I slipped a shell into it one day, set it in a corner of the attic, and forgot it. Sometime later Frank and I were playing there. He picked up the shotgun, cocked it, pointed it at me, and said, "You're dead." There is a blurred photograph of J. P. Alley holding that same gun in the crook of his arm. It had a hair trigger. My brother tossed it onto a mattress in the half-light of the attic, and it went off and blew away a section of the window frame, leaving Frank looking wan and extremely contemplative. It took me fifteen years to admit to Dad that I had loaded the gun. Meanwhile, at age twelve, I used it for its intended purpose.

Bud drove a pink and white Ford Fairlane convertible with skirts on the fenders for that sleek, impregnable look, and a muffler that blew unlawfully loud exhaust. The rear bumper hovered within inches of the road; dried mud and grass clung to the trailer hitch. Inside, old tarpaulin, decoys, shotgun shells, jumper cables, and hip boots piled on the imitation white leather detracted from the car's suaveness; dust lay thickly on the dash and its four-battery flashlight and bubble compass. Stuffed above the visors were licenses and scribbled, barely literate permissions to tromp on land relatively few people knew existed. The smells of gasoline and the muddy immensity of the Mississippi slipped through the gaps between the windows and the patched cloth top.

The owner of the car was in most ways the antithesis of my father. Bud represented a version of the southern male close to ubiquitous, however, and his world a basic alternative to the mundane and the civilized that Memphis seemed so proud of. His Ford was often parked behind the gas station down the street, next to a little silver Airstream where Bud slept. He was about thirty, a case of arrested development whose father owned the station. Bud helped out when he wasn't earning good money at the Fruehauf plant, or off in the country. Rawboned, with close-cropped black hair plastered to his head by sweatbands and thin lips that pinched the ever-present Camel, Bud treated my mother politely when servicing our green Hudson; he gave us a duck on occasion, or a catfish, totems from that other world. My father liked Bud but pointed out that he wasn't "going anywhere," that hunting and fishing four and five days a week was excessive even by southern standards.

Bud treated the kids who hung around his father's station like equals, which in many ways we were. Periodically he took them hunting. I badly wanted to go, and my father's counterarguments — that twelve-year-olds were too young, that we owned no hunting gear — were no match for my ardor. I went to bed one night in thin December light and watched the darkness come on, the merciful beginning of something that had to end before something else could get under way. I was buzzed awake at three A.M. by the alarm clock, and crawled into borrowed clothes. Then I was eating a waffle — an extravagance — in the glare of the Toddle House lights. Bud and I headed for Arkansas in the Fairlane, our destination Coca-Cola's duck-hunting preserve near Stuttgart, a flooded fiefdom surrounded by a moat and patrolled by private guards.

Bud believed in taking what was available, not theft exactly but a sharing in bountiful nature. Property and legality were, to him, matters of individual interpretation. "You've got to get yours," he said, "yours" being whatever you could get away with taking, a piece of the good life that would never be handed to you.

We got ours by first teetering along dead trees that had

fallen across Coke's moat, wearing heavy rubber hip boots and carrying shotguns, a crazy exercise. To slip was to drown, or at least catch pneumonia. There was a skin of ice on the water, gray under gray skies. Bud launched his calls into them, chuffing on the wooden tube while we listened to the corporate sports shooting from heated blinds farther in. I was squatting on the upheaved roots of a felled oak, relieving myself, when the first mallards came; I raised the shotgun, pulled the trigger, and almost went over with the force of the kick.

A bead of blood depended at the tip of the drake's beak, as luminous as the green head feathers. I carried the body in my jacket, a warm lump of guilt, a reluctant miracle.

A year later Bud quit his job at Fruehauf and built a plywood shack buoyed by empty oil drums on a lonely stretch of river upstream, tethered in flooded willows at the tip of an island called Brandywine. For ages the Mississippi had formed great loops in the land, confusing state boundaries by breaking through to new channels, leaving dry lagoons and brackish oxbows where mosquitoes bred and armored gars floated on moonlit nights. In isolated woodlots on Brandywine the poison ivy grew fan-like leaves and hummocked roots; big stands of oak, hickory, and walnut remained uncut, the deer, wild turkeys, and razorback hogs unhunted. The interior of the island had harbored a penal colony in the early years of the century but the settlement was long gone, pulled down by creepers and violent rains.

Bud's shack was anchored on the edge of the mile of doghair willow, in what had once been the main channel. No one seemed to know if it was in Arkansas or Tennessee, or to care. He paid no rent and no taxes. Expansion depended solely on the availability of empty oil drums, and Bud became the only man on the lower Mississippi who owned two floating beagle packs. He used one for hunting rabbits, one for deer. Brandywine provided country big enough to swallow you; eventually the river would loom among trees so capacious they shut out the sun, an expanse of water and silt carried down from mysterious headwaters toward Vicksburg and New Orleans, plowed by saurian monsters urging pencil-thin lines of barges toward Cairo and St. Louis.

Brandywine did have an inhabitant, an old half-breed named Monk, with skin like stretched rawhide and a perpetually dripping nose. He lived in a tent with a wood-burning stove and several feists, muscular little dogs that were hell on squirrels I knocked out of the tops of oaks with J. P. Alley's old single-barrel. Monk was paid by a rich man in Memphis, who owned the island, to keep people from hunting there. Bud brought Monk whiskey, canned milk, and other necessities from town, shot craps with him on a greasy blanket spread in front of the tent, along with hands from the tugs who came ashore to carouse, and Bud was awarded the island as his private preserve.

Once Bud put me ashore on the other side of Brandywine and told me to walk to Monk's. "Just head into the sun," he would say, or, "If you hit the willows, turn left. You can't get lost." I imagined annihilation in the dense tangles of creeper and sassafras, under the tusks of wild hogs that left great swaths of moist, uprooted earth. They were too canny to be seen and no real threat, yet stories of boars ripping open the stomachs of pursuing hounds had made a deep impression. I came across deer on their day beds, and in April a spawn of water moccasins emerging from hibernation: thick, black hanks of scales with flat heads and evil eyes, too besotted with sleep to strike. Then the river would appear among the trees with the force of salvation. In Monk's squalid, packed-dirt courtyard, men would be rolling dice on hands and knees, in their fists dollars and the passed-around, sloshing pint.

*

A speedboat sits at Bud's dock, an old Chris-Craft with the varnish gone, the two hunters behind the cloudy windshield watching our approach. In the evenings passers-by often came to talk and drink coffee made from boiled river water, sitting in dilapidated chairs around Bud's table. The place smelled of the lantern's exhaust and contained, if ducks were stewing, a feral delectation that hung two feet below the ceiling. The sounds of scraping boots, yapping dogs, and the voices of men unmoored from their women filled the place.

This time there is something wrong. I step onto the dock and tie up the skiff, proud of this ability, and Bud asks one of the hunters, "Do any good?"

The man says, "Shot himself."

I see the third one then, sprawled in the stern, a jacket over his head. A hand protrudes, freckled with blood.

"Shoving his gun under the seat, by the barrel."

I am afraid I will topple into the water. Carefully I crouch, my back against the cabin, while the men talk, their pale faces etched into the dun backdrop of willow whips. There is a grainy tangibility about the sky; I do not want to look at the thing in the back of the boat, but I do, struck most by its stillness.

Bud took up commercial fishing. He used hoop nets he wove himself and dropped into the river, tied to anchors; the current held them open and into them swam the most amazing things. As one of several boys who worked for Bud one summer, I raised the nets, collected fish, and helped peddle them to the tugs. We also hawked fish in Orange Mound, one of Memphis's black neighborhoods, where customers pointed out the fish they wanted, and I would haul it out and flop it into the pan on the scale, and Bud would calculate the price. He carried a notebook in the back pocket of his jeans in which he kept track of money owed him by gaunt men in worn wing-tips who laughed and bargained, by big-breasted women and sometimes girls.

Later, he would ask me, "You like that poontang?"

We sold what was left of the haul to a monger in a rubber apron on Summer Avenue, who slithered the fish across his slimy concrete slab while I tried to wash the stench from my hands. No girl of any color would pay attention to an evil-smelling fisherman's apprentice, even one operating out of the trunk of a pink convertible.

The riskiness of the fishing appealed to me. I was a free agent in what struck most people as a remote, even hostile place. Nothing moved on that broad canvas of woods and water I couldn't claim. The muscles in my arms acquired defining ridges; my skin turned nut brown. Several times a day I jumped into, and even drank, water most Memphians were reluctant to touch. The fishermen who appeared on weekends to toss out lines attached to cans — "jugs" — and float amidst their litter, drinking beer and getting sunburned, watched me with what I imagined to be respect. I was the native, knife strapped on, capable of stealing their fish, their coolers, and maybe their daughters.

I memorized the nets' locations, trees on shore my guides. I would swing the grappling hook overhead, heave it into the water, watch the line play out, feel the metal tines catch. I hauled hand over hand, turning the skiff into the current, using the gunwale as a fulcrum. The net rose through opacity. Bud wanted catfish, but I yearned for gars; there were stories of twelve-footers wriggling through the shallows to drag off human babies, and even the small ones ripped holes in the mesh as they escaped. But sometimes the net jammed between their translucent teeth, sharp as needles, drowning them, and these I could examine at leisure, poking at the eyes and tweaking the teeth, before dumping the whole primordial mess back into the river.

Once Dad drove me up to the landing, inside the levee in Arkansas, and we all fished for crappie on a backwater. He enjoyed this, as he did any activity exclusively male, but the scene was too elemental for him. Bud's cabin represented commendable independence but also a rejection of society that included, Dad rightly suspected, some lawlessness. The renegade's was not his version of individualism. On the other hand, I was learning things Dad couldn't teach me, and not pestering him to take me into places where he wasn't entirely capable.

One day when we were alone, Bud said, "That old gal's coming up tomorrow."

His taste in women was similar to his taste in cars: he liked them flashy, used, a bit dangerous. He could be picky. He had dropped a good-looking blond waitress because she allowed food to accumulate in the cracks in her Formica tabletop. This new woman, Karen, was divorced; he had taken her water-skiing in cloacal McKeller Lake, in south Memphis, where she had snuggled up to him in the water, and later they had gotten naked in his Airstream. Bud hinted that Karen might make her ravenous self available to me, too. Extending his woods ethic, he said that using a woman to help a friend get his was just like using your car to smuggle a friend's ducks past the game warden, concealed under hubcaps.

The next day Karen appeared in the bow of Bud's skiff — large, pretty, her streaked blond hair tied up in a scarf. Bud said, "Say hello to Karen, Jim."

There were little gaps between her teeth. The raised heels on her plastic sandals made her step from the boat awkward; the shorts cut into the tops of full, downy thighs. The halter showed cleavage that didn't disappear when she straightened up.

Karen took in the willow thicket, the radiant tin roof under the ferocious sun, and said, "My, my."

I followed her inside, where she glanced at the boots and nets, clothes hanging from nails, the strikingly clutter-free double bed, and added, "This is real cute."

Bud produced the Thermos of ice, gin, and lemonade, and took down two jelly glasses. Karen asked me, "What do you do up here?"

"He runs the nets," said Bud. "Jim could tell you a thing or two about the river. Here, try this on for size."

They drank while I lay on my cot and pretended to read *Field and Stream* ("Hairy Lures for Monster Bass"). I went swimming and made noise doing it, hoping Karen would join me, but she stayed out of the sun. Only when the angle of the roof had thrown a shadow over the dock did she come outside, and then she wanted to ride in the skiff. She insisted upon sitting in the stern — I could have told her the boat wouldn't plane — and when they came back her arm was around Bud's neck.

"Aren't you gonna run the nets?" she asked me.

The windows were propped open but the heat hung inside. Nothing moved on our glassy backwater. Bud poured me a glass of his concoction and I took it outside and sipped it with exaggerated nonchalance. Karen sat on the edge of the dock, sandals off, her feet in the water, listening to the radio. Mosquitoes courting in the cottonwoods along the bank made more noise than the Grand Ole Opry. Bud sang along with the song, changing the words slightly: "'Jimbo, Jimbo, where you gonna go-ee-o? Jimbo, Jimbo, what'cha gonna do-ee-o?'"

I could see rivulets of sweat running down between Karen's breasts, leaving tiny furrows in the blond hairs. I tried not to let her catch me looking, but the heat and the gin had made me stupid.

"'. . . does your mommy knoooow, you're going down the road to see a little girl-ee-o?'"

Karen asked, "How old are you?"

"Fourteen."

"You must get bored without anybody your own age around. I'd flat get bored."

Supper consisted of Dinty Moore beef stew and canned peaches. The two of them kept drinking. Afterward, Karen pulled Bud to his feet and jitterbugged to the music. I was surprised that a big woman could move so well. Her cantilevered breasts swung back and forth; I had never seen anything like them — they had a life of their own, operating on some new principle of levitation. I heard Bud say, "You try, Jim."

Karen caught me by the arm and swung me into her. I had slow danced in the cafeteria at school and was no stranger to the pelvic thrust, but nothing had prepared me for Karen's unabashed proximity. Her left breast padded my collarbone; she slipped her fingers into the hair on the back of my neck and moved me around the floor. I felt the unexpected compactness of her waist above those hips, and below, her soft belly and that tight reality.

Bud said, "Bedtime."

He stripped to his boxer shorts, turned off the Coleman, and stretched out on the double bed. I undressed, listening to the lantern's gasp, my back to Karen. I went outside to brush my teeth — the dutiful hygienist. The sordidness of all this didn't escape me; I was ashamed of it, as I was of killing game out of season and other schemes to get yours, but the prospect of Karen overwhelmed that. On some level I knew my time on the river was over and that this sexual setup would not be repeated.

She lay on her back next to Bud, still in her shorts. In the near-darkness I could see that the halter was gone but not the bra, and exposed female underwear of any sort was unprecedented. Women lived on an astral plane; most of what I knew about them was hearsay. Dad had not explained the facts of life to me; his code left no room for embarrassing specifics. A man, even a young one, gained that kind of knowledge by masculine osmosis. Dad sometimes looked at women on the street in a way that troubled me, preoccupied, but they and their anatomy weren't the subjects of conversation. He didn't tell dirty jokes, the main source of my sex education, augmented by *Cavalier* and the usual dirty palaver among boys who pursued the real thing in fantasy — at home, on the bus, in the Normal Theater where jackets were spread like inverted trampolines washed in the reflected glow of Esther Williams and Natalie Wood.

I lay down beside her. Almost immediately Bud began to snore, genuine rafter-shakers that made the pretense of sleep impossible. Karen sighed: fatigue, exasperation, or lust. Emboldened by the dancing but extremely tentative, I turned and touched her arm; she didn't move it, and I touched her stomach. This was warm and damp, rising and falling, evidence I assumed of a divorcée's passion. I inched my hand upward until it arrived, daringly, on a compacted mound of breast. The heft amazed me. With what I thought was great discretion I began to search for the peak of that arching mass, expecting Karen to move my hand, or to make a comment, even to help, but she did nothing at all.

I passed over the top of the bra and began to tunnel, tricky because of the angle and the unyielding material. Elbow in the air, I worked deeper, across the soft topography of the ultimate bareness. I imagined a nipple rising, and thought I detected a tremor of encouragement. Then my hand got stuck. It felt like coathanger wire; freer access was prevented by the bra clasp, buried beneath all those square inches of a woman who inhaled so deeply it hurt. I worked my hand free and went for the shorts instead, trussed in front with strings I had studied in daylight, intimidated by their complexity. When my fingers were deep in that thicket, Karen again sucked air, and the laces went taut.

I didn't know what to do next. It occurred to me that we might discuss this dilemma, but Karen clearly didn't want a conversation with some kid in the middle of nowhere. I had been defeated by her formidable hydraulics.

Bud came awake and reached for her, and Karen whispered, "Not here."

They went outside to argue. I heard the Evinrude start up and went to the door. By then the skiff was an outbound wedge on moonlit water, Karen in the bow, facing away from the coal of Bud's cigarette. They ran over a gar — *thwup* — and disappeared under the dark lee of Arkansas.

9

AUNT ELIZABETH and Uncle Frank belonged to the Memphis Country Club, just one collection of worthy Memphians, but *the* one. Sometimes in the summer I would be invited there, to play with my cousins in the tepid, azure depths of the pool and later to wolf down a hamburger in the shade of an umbrella. The Conaways couldn't afford even the surrogate clubs of Memphis, named for Memphis's Indians (Chickasaw), the glorious past (Colonial), and so on. Smaller but as exclusive as the MCC was the Hunt and Polo Club, where for some reason the preferred activities were not hunting and polo but drinking and bridge.

On Thanksgiving, members of the various clubs gathered in dining rooms overlooking golf courses, white cloths, and heavy flatware, to be served drinks — the standards — by black men in red jackets who made those places function more by reassurance than efficiency. We rarely saw those serving tables that offered fruit compotes full of marshmallows, pickled things in bright colors, slabs of tomato aspic, mashed potatoes and creamed onions, domestic quail cooked to total, toothsome acquiescence, turkey, stuffing, cranberry doubloons, barges of dark pan gravy, and always sweet salad dressings, crackers in cellophane, and apple, pecan, and mince pies with cobbles of ice cream.

Whiskey by the drink was illegal in Memphis, but not at the clubs, one of many contradictions no one ever talked about. To bring up these subjects was somehow to question them. The same silence applied to claims we were expected to accept: that Memphis was both the cleanest and the quietest city in the world and that it contained the biggest Baptist church anywhere. What would have been a source of pride in an Episcopal church was merely a curiosity in a Baptist one, Baptists being looked down upon not because so many Baptists were black but because Baptist meant country.

Methodists were better, although they sang too much. Some Methodists were "attractive," a vague term used by my mother and my aunt to distinguish between those of all religions who were acceptable and those who weren't. Attractive people had the right comportment and knew what to laugh at, and understood veiled references to other attractive people. That didn't necessarily mean they were the "right people," a higher accolade. Very few Methodists were the right people, for instance, a fact that Dodo considered irrelevant. She occasionally attended the big Methodist church across the street, whose parishioners stuck their Fords and Buicks in our broad driveway, emboldened by the presence of God and the knowledge that my father wouldn't have them towed on a Sunday.

The next rung up was occupied by Presbyterians. Here things got complicated. You had social Presbyterians and then you had the righteous sorts who did not drink and could offer rational arguments as to why not. It seemed to me that Presbyterians had the highest, pointiest steeples in Memphis. There were quite a few attractive Presbyterians, many of whom were the right people, but it was better to be Episcopalian. They drank without regret, and the pomp of their services made Presbyterianism look anemic.

We attended St. John's Episcopal, where my brother and then I were acolytes. We carried the tapers and then the flag and eventually the cross, heralded on Easter by trumpets ("Hail ye fes-ti-val *daaaaay* . . ."), under the most beautiful murals in town. A muscular blond Christ overspread the wall of the sacristy, with a phalanx of fair-skinned apostles at His feet. Leaving church, we passed beneath God Himself, a bearded Anglo-Saxon with an expression of mild, all-knowing disapproval. For me, it was less the face of divinity than that of the supreme adult, ruler of earth and sky. Adults had defeated Hitler and polio; they had invented television.

Outside the Protestant hierarchy existed a couple of other categories, like Catholicism, a troubling phenomenon. There were attractive Catholics, with some of the right people among them, but Catholics owed allegiance to a Mediterranean potentate. Their rituals were uncomfortably close to Episcopal ones but separated by the act of confession. Why would people confess to things they thought and did when thinking and doing those things wasn't necessarily their fault? And there were Jews, sometimes attractive but never the right people. Jews had their own country club, Ridgeway. They could play ball and go to parties, but there was a ceiling. The fact that Jews helped keep the engines of commerce and culture pumping made little impression on attractive Memphians.

None of these distinctions mattered much at Normal Training, but the school went only through the ninth grade, and then they would matter, when a high school had to be chosen and my feet more firmly set on an attractive path. Meanwhile, life at Training had been complicated by the arrival of a new principal, Mr. Christian, to replace the taciturn but kind one I had known since first grade. Mr. Christian's trousers were reined in over an ample stomach by a belt with an inscribed gold buckle; he ran soft hands over his glistening hair while humiliating students. During assembly he would call out the names of miscreants. He interrupted classes for this, to extricate boys for beatings, and even chased one across campus.

I didn't understand it then, but I was witnessing the triumph of the educational administrator over the practitioner. The teachers could not object to Mr. Christian's tactics; I saw a new misgiving in their faces akin to my own dread of the man. He was destined for a better job at the Board of Education, after first logging this experience. I gripped my ankles in the closeness of his office and shortstopped a board swung by his hands; the pain wasn't as bad as the impossibility of appeal. Mr. Christian was always right, and if by some unavoidable subversion of events he happened to be proved wrong, then the perpetrator of the proof was guilty of an even more grievous transgression, disrespect. All of this went down on your permanent record.

My father may not have approved of tyranny, but almost any dispute between adults and children should be resolved, in his eyes, in favor of the adult. Juvenile delinquency was considered a communicable disease. Once, on a business trip to Nashville with my father, where I spent hours sitting in the offices of sheet metal and compressor manufacturers, I found the chance to secretly buy a switchblade knife at a pawnshop. Back in Memphis, I sold it for a profit to a gawky boy named Tyrone. Unfortunately his mother discovered the knife, and returned it to my house. I had never seen my father so angry. Not only did I have to return the money but I had to stand by, in the front yard, scared speechless, while he assaulted the knife with a hammer; I can still hear steel ringing against steel, on the steppingstone, can see bits of bone handle flying and that broad, bright blade breaking like a piece of crockery.

*

Coincident with Mr. Christian's time at Normal Training School and in many ways complementary to it was the reign of Coach Fulgum, who had played first-string guard all four years in college, a fact that retained for him a profound importance. This gave Fulgum the right to pronounce at will on the human condition and affirmed the universal goodness of football. As Training's commander of all sports, Fulgum had simply exchanged locker rooms, moving from Memphis State (formerly the teachers' college), the aboveground haunt of meaty stars like himself, to Training's sweaty, subterranean cell of teenagers uneasy about our abilities, our standing in the world, and the size of our penises, most of us lacking, in Fulgum's view, the nimbus of the eternal starter.

He told us about the plays and runbacks of yesteryear as if he were still on the gridiron accomplishing the impossible. He spent hours in the cage at the end of our locker room, amidst hanging shoulder pads and jockstraps, making lists of issued equipment, of first and second teams, and of students who lacked the proper appreciation of the sport of their coach. That list was in Fulgum's head, and you didn't want to get on it because, once there, you couldn't get off. He also taught hygiene. Fulgum's directives on the human body were unchallengeable, derived from personal observation and deduction. Brushing your hair twice a day prevented baldness. Sleeping on your back with your legs rigidly extended increased height. Masturbation engendered pimples. During these fulminations all signs of inattention or disrespect on the part of students were met with the same admonition: "You have twenty-eight teeth in your head. Would you like to try for none?"

Apparently the only thing unrelated to sports Coach Fulgum had ever learned was a stanza from Macaulay's "Horatius at the Bridge." In the middle of a class on nutrition he recited:

Then out spake brave Horatius,
The Captain of the Gate:
"To every man upon this earth
Death cometh soon or late.
And how can man die better
Than facing fearful odds
For the ashes of his fathers
And the temples of his Gods . . ."

This wasn't to praise poetry or heroism but to prove that drinking quarts of milk empowered memory.

I carried real baggage in Fulgum's eyes: my brother's name was on his list of undesirables. Frank had been a good basketball player, but that wasn't enough to get him on Fulgum's first team because Frank hadn't played football, too. First string was reserved for football players, whatever their talents in basketball. The first string was usually losing when Fulgum put in the second string to save the game, and my brother revealed his impatience with this custom by bouncing the ball off the coach's commanding profile during a practice session.

Frank moved on to Central High but his sin was familial. I didn't help myself any, my first year in junior high, by being flippant ("Jim, you have twenty-eight teeth in your head . . .") and too light for anything but third-string quarterback. In basketball, I played as a substitute in the eighth grade but not enough, in Fulgum's view, for a letter. Track marshaled my talents and anxieties into bursts of competitive effort that were in a way scarier than football, leaving me with a single objective and no cover. Track did strange and painful things to my body; it revealed clear limits and left a residue of satisfaction not totally dependent upon winning. I discovered second wind in the quarter mile, and the ceiling of propulsion just short of the finish line, when my lungs seemed to collapse and my legs came up like rusty steel risers and I watched older boys from the wrong side of the tracks, with nascent mustaches and more stamina, wheel past.

Fulgum recognized my effort in track but ruled that I was a race short of a letter. My father went to talk to him about it. I imagine a slight, impatient man in the right confronting a slab of competitive pomposity like Fulgum, and feel sorry for Dad. The visit didn't affect my place in Fulgum's mental calculations or on the playing fields.

By the time I reached the ninth grade I had been looking at Coach Fulgum for roughly half my life, an impediment of sorts. That fall I dropped out of the football lineup after he put my name on both the varsity and second-team lists, a deft put-down but a useful introduction to the absurd. I was dating a cheerleader named Ann, and after school instead of sweating in pads and jersey I would lie in the Johnson grass and watch Ann and her friends practice, their heavy flared skirts riding up on the centrifugal force of the most strenuous celebrations of football, revealing tight shorts in Training's institutional blue. My reveries involved lust and a sweet approximation of guilt, since I wasn't out in the September sun with the rest of the team.

Go back, go back,
Go back into the woods
Because, because
You haven't got the goods.

When the girls were done they removed their cheerleading skirts and walked home with them draped over their shoulders. The sight of Ann's muscular legs, enhanced by a summer tan, stopped the action dead on the football field, where Fulgum's displeasure was etched into the white sky like a face on a counterfeit nickel. He watched us walk toward the waterworks, where Ann and I would make out under the cover of magnolias and I gradually forgot the quarterback sneak and double reverse.

With spring had come an entirely new reality, one that had little to do with sports and nothing whatsoever to do with Training. Future glory resided in something larger and more compelling, known as frats.

My father had belonged to a high school fraternity; so had my brother. Frank had been president of Tau Delta Tau, letters that stood for nothing but retained an almost supernatural power in the minds of members and aspirants: strange, spiny symbols that meant the difference between a good life and one of ignominy. Identical Greek brotherhoods in Memphis, and the sisterhoods, threw the best parties, provided endless social grazing, and served as social winnowers. This custom, irrelevant today, involved a complexity of tribal affiliation worthy of an anthropologist and illustrates, I think, the obsessions of an age of prescribed group behavior.

Joined at the top with Tau — "Taw" — were other fraternities pandemic in appeal, their members coming from several different high schools, all on the right side of the tracks. First you had to be rushed, a process of evaluation that began with a phone call from a fraternity member who picked you up in his car, with his date, drove you to pick up your date and then to the Rainbow Terrace Room. There, other fraternity members approached, shook your hand, looked into your eyes, and talked about ball and who you knew. After midnight you all crossed town to a big house in east Memphis for bacon and eggs, and finally you sat alone in your room, grappling with your tie and wondering what impression you had made.

In some ways I was the perfect candidate. My brother had been president. I knew how to dress and how to act and seemed to understand the crucial difference between being merely polite and being cool. The latter involved timing as much as anything, a delayed reaction to social stimuli that suggested wit and experience, even when you had none, and a profound awareness of the exalted but unspoken male role.

Coolness implied guts. It was exclusive, a cosmic weighing of alternatives followed by the sure selection of a course of action reflecting well on the selector and his organization. Coolness entailed an awareness of music, cars — models, not the mechanical stuff — and sports. Coolness was the difference between outright snobbery and a considered, droll expression of God-given superiority. Advanced cool suggested an acceptance of Fate in human affairs — irony around the edges of conversation, a steadiness in voice and motion. It was getting laid and alluding to the fact without describing anything. It was itself — you couldn't fake it.

Except that, of course, you could. I knew this, too. Sports meant less to me than I pretended; I was afraid a lot of the time — of rejection by girls, of missing out on something impossible to define, of getting beaten up in the pugilistic theater that was teenage Memphis. I dressed in imitation of my big brother. My conversational gambits tended to be skittish and off-the-wall, in part because my voice cracked. I didn't respond well to coolness directed against me, although no response could be interpreted as the ultimate expression of cool. Generally this was a distillation of various notions of acceptable male behavior, with a touch of modulated rebellion; it celebrated belonging, the highest objective of a man in Memphis. I had been prepared for fraternity life in principle. Dad had the attributes and interests of a country club member, but he didn't belong to one; he taught Frank and me to play golf and tennis, rather than to fish, but didn't provide access to golf courses and courts that many of our friends had. I knew that my immediate family had no hand in "running" Memphis, but somehow we belonged anyway. These activities proved it.

*

One Sunday a Buick wheeled into our driveway and older boys piled out; there under the oak they urged me to accept a bid to Tau, as if I might refuse. We careened through the streets, horn blaring, picked up another rushee, and finally pulled up in front of a large, pillared house in Chickasaw Gardens. All around us fraternities and sororities were going through the same process. Girls' lives were complicated by the existence of both sororities and clubs — Four Seasons, Decem, Chez Nous, Sunev (Venus spelled backward) — and subject to unwritten rules. Their cars passed with banners flying, the occupants singing sacred songs. Open convertibles held medleys of lipstick, white collars, circle pins, and pleated skirts. Girls sat on the trunks, and one lay with her hair spread over the polished hood. The cars stopped in front of a house and girls streamed over the lawn and clamored at the door until yet another girl appeared, and shrieked, and they all rode off, still singing. There were stories of those calls being made to the wrong house, and of girls and boys waiting for bids that never came. I would see in their faces on Monday morning that they had been affected in a basic way, that certain possibilities were forever behind them.

Later, members of Tau drove the new pledges through the parking lot of Willie King's, where couples feeding from trays attached to the sills of cars looked at us with what I imagined to be deep respect. Willie King's was a forum for imagined coolness, a place to eat and dally, and to be seen doing so; mostly it served as a quasi-public arena for whatever sort of behavior you thought you could get away with, and as a smorgasbord of potential but generally unrealized sexual encounters heavy with auto exhaust and skittering music from wheeled radio dials. There were other such places — the Jungle Inn, Town and Country — but Willie King's represented the apex.

Pledges' backgrounds might differ but we all held to something larger, or thought we did. Without that feeling of belonging we could never have put up with the demands of the same members who had been so nice to us. We could not have produced so many little wooden paddles sanded to absolute silkiness, painted white and sanded again, then fitted with the initials TΔT, carved from balsa wood with deep concentration and painted royal purple. The tiny paddles were strung from the mirrors of members' cars, symbolic of the real versions we fashioned from barrel staves and brought to meetings each Sunday at two in the afternoon, following the other rituals of church and family dinner.

The real paddles were broken against our backsides. The trick was to make the handles sufficiently weak so they broke after a few blows, but not weak enough to shatter immediately, which would bring on more beating. Pledges were called into meetings and ordered to recite ritual, to make love to a Coke bottle, or to tell a dirty joke. In those smoky arenas boys a few years older than I seemed grown, slumped in easy chairs and arrayed on the windowsills, joking and laughing; they slipped effortlessly from fraternal good will to frenzied abuse that was to culminate in initiation, a prospect too horrible to contemplate. But if you could survive it, you might wear the Tau Delta Tau pin, a black enamel diamond edged with seed pearls and attached by a tiny gold chain to a gold omega — the Memphis chapter. We pledges were all certain the fraternity pin would find its way onto a girl's sweater, at the very tip of a breast irresistibly attracted to it.

Our final Sunday as pledges we were given a list that included a dozen paddles, a gallon of used motor oil, five pounds of sawdust, a quart of molasses, a dozen eggs, and a bag of elephant dung. My mother drove me and some friends to the zoo, where we stood in silence while a black man in rubber boots shoveled what he assured us was elephant dung into burlap sacks. He never asked what we intended to do with it, and we didn't tell him. The night of initiation I waited in the front yard, in old clothes, for the same car that had brought me a bid months before. It pulled up with three fraternity brothers sitting in the front seat and, in the back seat, a friend of mine known as Rughead and another pledge. I loaded my collection into the trunk and slid in next to them. We rode east in silence, past Second Presbyterian, past the section known as White Station, and Memorial Cemetery, the city dwindling into the broad meadows of Germantown, neatly fenced, ghostly. We turned south on a dirt road and joined a caravan of cars that crossed into the piney flats of north Mississippi.

We passed shacks and finally stopped in a circle of headlights far from any sign of human habitation. The pledges unloaded the malodorous cargoes while members handed 'round cans of beer, laughing in a way that made my mouth go cottony. First came the beating. We bent over at a sufficient distance from other pledges to allow members the maximum stroke. The blows were languorous at first, then more enthusiastic; the woods resounded with what might have been a mounting military skirmish. We were told to strip, and the members ran us in a circle in our underpants. An egg broke against the back in front of me, another against my head, and soon each of us gleamed with slithering raw protein.

We were caught one by one, pulled aside, and beaten some more while being anointed with molasses. We were pushed to our knees; I felt the warm, viscous envelope of motor oil about my head, followed by a storm of sawdust. I collided with the boy in front of me and sat gasping, glimpsing other dumb, filthy beasts and the crazy line of members' legs silhouetted by the headlights. I was afraid — of the members' loss of control, more frightening than the pain they inflicted, of giving way to some really horrible demand, of bawling. All notions of coolness, of inner masculine reserve that supposedly got people through such things, were gone. We pledges were kids again and the members adults, without the pretense of fair play or good will.

The elephant dung had been emptied into one pile. We were herded toward it and forced to crawl around in this soft, noxious climax of all our social ambition. We ended up in the trunks of cars, or in back seats on tarpaulins, to be driven home and to stand, in the early morning hours, dabbing at ourselves with rags soaked in paint thinner.

By Sunday we were clean again, ready for the final rite, performed in another house in Chickasaw Gardens by frat officers wearing special robes. In a dark room our sponsors stood behind us and attested to our worth; we mouthed the ritual we had been memorizing for months, and it was over. We were Taus. Our new brothers pulled the drapes aside; sunlight flooded the room, and the president said "Congratulations, men" to relieved and unutterably proud fifteen-year-olds.

10

IN THE FIFTIES, the "right" Memphians weren't overly concerned with any music heard outside a church. There were more churches in Memphis than gas stations, or so we were told. W. C. Handy's trumpet had reverberated on Beale Street, lined with storefronts and cafés in a neighborhood that still smelled of charred hickory and the residue of barbecue sauces locally divined and applied with paintbrushes. Occasionally some blues slipped past the rusty screen doors of black bars, but white people went to Beale Street during the day only for passport photos or to rent a tuxedo or to trade an old railway watch for cash under the three dangling brass balls. Pawnshops stood in direct opposition to the prevailing notion of suburban rectitude.

The city would eventually get around to naming a square on Beale for Handy; many of the buildings would be razed and brought up again in architectural fantasies of what had existed before the entertainment was canned and the food franchised. Meanwhile the rest of downtown was being abandoned by whites. They still attended parties at the Peabody Hotel, where the Mississippi Delta was said to begin, and men in seersucker still passed beneath ornate façades of Front Street and into the old cotton emporiums, but their purpose was more and more real estate speculation and less and less the product for which the Deep South was famous.

The refurbishment of Main Street as one long shopping strip would fail to call back those citizens who had shifted eastward; it would become known unofficially as the Nairobi Mall. Today Graceland, farther from the river, lies in a welter of commercialism catering to tourists, on a street locals call Suicide Boulevard, where may be bought objects as various as Toyotas and the Graceland Coin Purse. Drivers slow down to rubberneck the music reliquaries and run into one another, hence the nickname.

Handy was not the pride of white Memphis, but then neither was Elvis, not in the fifties when he was beginning to gain a national reputation. Elvis wasn't a star here; he was a greaseball from Tupelo. His debt to black music couldn't be obscured by a message that was Caucasian, Protestant, transcendent, echoing through white fundamentalist congregations all over the South. A case could be made for Heartbreak Hotel as a fleabag purgatory for poor white boys like Elvis himself, his music ephemeral by virtue of his origins. It reached our ears over *Red, Hot and Blue*, a raunchy radio broadcast ruled by a countrified DJ whose Falstaff beer commercials were as well known as his choice of music: "Freeze it and eat it! Open up a rib and pour it in!" This would be followed by Roy Orbison's "Pretty Woman" or one of the inspirations of Killer Diller Lewis.

Memphis acquired Elvis as it acquired many of its citizens, by Greyhound or Trailways, rusty pickup or low-slung sedan, rolling in from the sweltering hinterland; the city processed him through one of the segregated schools beyond the frontiers of respectability, Humes High, where Elvis's classmates had names like Duane, Gavin, and Merle. Their hair glistened; they had an apparently genetic understanding of the internal combustion engine. We called them rogues and looked apprehensively but with wonder at their cars, more affected by gravity than ours, the smoothly rounded surfaces deprived of chrome and bright emblems of automotive distinction, reflecting an opalescent, homegrown individuality. Whenever we sighted one of these machines, we chanted, "Chopped, channeled, lowered, Offenhauser heads. Chopped, channeled, lowered, Offenhauser . . . ," without understanding exactly what the words meant.

In stripping away mid-century ornamentation, the drivers had made their cars into expressions of mechanical rage — super-ambulatory, highly sonorous, exclusively white badassedness. Their mufflers — "glass packs" and "cutouts" — barked in defiance of the law that had made Memphis the quietest city in the country, spraying aural spermatozoa over those broad, ordered streets. The drivers, like Elvis, carried packs of Luckies rolled in the sleeves of their T-shirts; knotty biceps hugged the polished doors as they careened from mid-city stoplights, their engines fitted with twice as many carburetors as Detroit thought appropriate. Mechanics' skills were perpetuated in shop class, whereas in our shop classes we made racks for our fathers' shotguns or tooled leather purses that our mothers shoved to the backs of their dresser drawers. Outwardly we scoffed at hoodlum transport, but secretly the customized cars' owners scared us east Memphis boys, and their dates drove us to damp, solitary dreams.

These girls were known to do things in the back seats that girls from Miss Hutchinson's school did not do in the back seats of our fathers' sedans. Their hard beauty and nasal intonations, picked up in Arkansas when they weren't picked up in Mississippi or west Tennessee, signified blatant accessibility. They were not just compliant but *receptive,* preordained for acts of desire by dim rural customs, whereas our girlfriends seemed bred to the two-step and the preparation of toast points.

Elvis was considered culturally dangerous by our parents, but he wasn't "bad" — an accolade meaning physically tough. In fact he was a little frail for Humes, where some really bad boys decided early on to protect Elvis and so became stars in their own right. Without them the Presley baby face wouldn't have survived until wrecked by pharmacology and meatloaf thirty years later.

My friends and I weren't Elvis fans but we heard the music so much that "Don't Be Cruel" can still make the hair stand up on the back of my neck. No one actually knew Elvis. We heard about him from unlikely people: the girl next door to me had a friend who dated a boy who had once been the backup driver for Elvis on a trip to Paducah. We heard rumors of Elvis's renting the fairgrounds and allowing his friends to ride the Whip and the roller coaster and eat Pronto Pups far into the balmy, cricket-laden night. We did know that Elvis shopped for pegged trousers and hairline belts at Lansky's, on Beale, and we sometimes wandered there among the shirts with collars that could not be buttoned down, not to buy but to soak up menace. Humesians with chipped teeth I had seen at the Rainbow Terrace Room picked fights and hit with a slope-shouldered, frightening know-how that broke noses and bounced heads off asphalt.

I saw Elvis in a red midget racer on Poplar Avenue one Sunday afternoon, wearing goggles, his long dark hair undisturbed by the gale. By then he had left behind the roadhouses where he had performed for people who brought their bottles along in paper bags and for whom fighting was often more attractive than listening. We didn't know those places then, being too young to have seen Elvis in his obscurity, but word of those nights endured. We heard that people had once laughed at Elvis, and waited in the parking lot to catch him after the show and teach him a lesson. The men had seen their wives, girlfriends, and daughters writhing to Elvis's melodic stroke; a persistent rumor featured him with a length of garden hose hanging down the inside of his pants leg, a notion so stark, so sexually blatant, that it took the breath away.

The closest thing to those roadhouses that I came to know were the Plantation Inn and the Cotton Club, in West Memphis. Both required crossing the Mississippi River to another state and another set of laws. These places pulsed with a mixture of country, blues, and rock 'n' roll. Men, women, boys, and girls drank liquor with impunity and adhered to each other like flypaper. "Breaking in" on a couple was a potentially violent maneuver. A trip to the toilet might involve a physical challenge, to be sidestepped by artful insults or simply by refusing to fight or, if you were lucky, by joining the spectators at a fight already under way. More than once I stood at the reeking enamel orifice, concentrating on the job, armpits slippery, silently cursing the leisurely function of my own clammy innards. I was glad to reenter, unharmed, that enormous, raucous, smoke-strewn room.

Class distinctions were at work, but no one used that term except in the phrase "low class," synonymous with "white trash." These were, to my mind, people you saw on porches up some defile in east Tennessee, or in the Ozarks. Those standing in the forefront of rural poverty near Memphis tended to be black. Negroes may have been the missing element in acknowledged Memphis, not necessarily below the rank of a white country boy like Elvis, but of another universe, and yet there was more affection for them than for some whites, a tacit recognition of Negroes' difficult past and a culture that grew up in artful opposition to the controlling one. People like Elvis, in his incubation, had no excuse for being unattractive. Blacks were often spoken of as their natural enemies, since obstreperous poor whites "need someone to look down on." This equated people at the economic bottom without having to be specific about it, condemning their antisocial behavior when some of the worst of that went on inside the Memphis Country Club.

Twenty years later, by chance, I was introduced to Elvis in Las Vegas, where I had been sent to write a magazine article about another entertainer, Sammy Davis, Jr. We both ended up in Elvis's dressing room, crowded with backup singers, managers, wardrobe people, and bodyguards. Elvis had exchanged his jumpsuit for a red Revolutionary War coat with epaulets; his thick black hair resembled the hair I remembered, but the bloated face was someone else's. He greeted Davis, and told no one in particular that he, Elvis, had given Davis the black sapphire he wore: "Tha biggest black sapphire ah ever saw for tha biggest black star ah know." Elvis added, "I want ya'll to see my new ring," and a loop of admiration formed around his splayed, bejeweled hand. "Now this here's a star ruby. You see plenty of star sapphires, but you don't see many star rubies . . . Get a spot!"

Elvis's valet appeared with a pair of white trousers decorated with turquoise. Sammy Davis said he would like to have a pair made for himself, and Elvis said, "I give ya my permission."

Elvis returned to his separate dressing compartment and the rest of us gathered around the bar in the main room. One of the bodyguards told of visiting Spiro Agnew, the vice president, and the discomfort Elvis's entourage felt at being temporarily relieved of their weapons. Elvis had presented Agnew with a gold-inlaid Magnum revolver with ivory handles. While the bodyguard talked, I watched Elvis, alone in his suite, sipping Perrier. Memphis had long since decided that Elvis was a star, not only because he had brought to the city fame that could be exploited, but because he chose to live there when he could easily have lived in Nashville, Hollywood, or

Vegas. The skinny sexual demiurge who had once threatened mid-southern domestic virtue was unimaginable in this pudgy darling of Nixon Republicans. Elvis's friends seemed less affected by his success. They drank bourbon and told stories. The men had capped teeth now and sported conventional jackets instead of shiny black ones without lapels. They no longer wore the hairline belts from Lansky's, but the way they stood — feet widespread, shoulders rolling — was pure, unabashed Humes High.

My brother was off at college during my high school years, and I was once again following in his tracks, this time at Central, a midtown educational fortress attended by whites from all over Memphis. My mother imagined me at Memphis University School, a private haven for scions bound eventually for Sewanee and Duke. MUS wasn't in the realm of possibility, but that didn't prevent us from discussing it at the table as if it were, my mother dismayed at our lack of privilege, Dad impatient, Dodo perplexed by any interest in the subject whatsoever, and Jack indifferent to all but the biscuits.

Frank had prepared the way for me at Central, too, before going on to the University of Tennessee in Knoxville. He had made good grades; teachers liked him. When he was caught by a Golden Gloves champion with the boxer's girlfriend and beaten up between the bumpers of two parked cars, he didn't seem bothered much. My father wanted him to be an engineer but admitted that, with his looks and social talent, Frank could have walked straight out of college and into the best insurance firm in the South. Frank's unlimited potential as a seller of term-life policies was the one thing Dad and Jack agreed upon, before Frank developed a disturbing interest in literature.

My brother Dan's earliest memory of him — Frank was thirteen years older than he — is of an adult sitting on the couch smoking cigarettes and reading novels. Frank may have been only five years older than I, but the practical distance between us, too, was immense. My dual roles of younger and older brother confused me; I wasn't the exemplar for Dan that Frank had been for me; my own misgivings about almost everything left little room for conscious example and sometimes for kindness, and Dan grew up good-natured but careful, with the wit of a partisan living in occupied territory.

Our extended family included no less than five Franks, two Calvins, an Uncle Jimmy, a Jimbo, and a Jimtoo. Underneath the alternately friendly and competitive relationship with our Chickasaw Gardens cousins lay Dad's financial struggle and Mom's ongoing but only alluded-to belief that the world was passing her by. She sometimes inadvertently set one of her brothers against the other — that wasn't hard to do — her boys against her husband, or any one of the males in the house against another. I feel sorry for her now, the only girl in a collection of boys, my father included, all of us dependent upon her and largely oblivious of that fact. When Dodo and Jack were traveling she was the only female in the house, with the exception of the part-time maid, and black people didn't count in gender or other questions.

Mom's femininity remained ardent, uncompromising, vulnerable. We believed in respectability, and yet my parents' fights must have equaled any in their intensity. Nothing was thrown, no one was hit, and yet they argued stridently over things as various as money and "respect," most of which made less sense to me than the anger and sometimes despair I saw on their faces. My father and mother — and consequently my brothers and I — were known for temperamental explosions that sent out blame like shrapnel, to be forgotten by the perpetrator with surprising speed and deftness. When young I once tried to mediate my parents' "squabble" and was let know by Dad that it was none of my business. A vague desolation hung about these differences. Mom threatened on occasion to walk out, and once or twice did take off for someone's house, and returned in embarrassingly poignant reconciliations. Dad was incapable of living by himself for more than a few minutes, and the shifting shades of resentment, love, and dependency on his face were as welcome to me as they were confusing.

About this time my mother decided to do something about the Lane nose, to have it brought into line with her notion of white American pulchritude; this became a subject of painful conversation rather than a tacit accomplishment that would have caused everyone less emotional hardship, particularly Mom. I think her sister had already undergone the operation, and my mother wanted one, too — an unusual bit of surgery in those days, in that place. Unfortunately my father valued the present configuration of my mother's nose as part of the larger reality, and didn't want to have to come to terms with another one, or to pay for it.

He returned home from work one evening, a week after the operation, to find my mother waiting for him on the back porch. The bandage was gone, as were the puffiness about her eyes and the traces of bruise. Unprepared for the revelation, probably reflecting on the sale of a piece of industrial equipment, Dad looked up at a woman who bore a strong resemblance to his wife. He didn't say anything.

"You don't like it," she sobbed, and then it was too late.

"Oh, honey . . ."

Mom sank to her knees, and it took Dad and Dodo to get her up again. But within a few days the new nose had obliterated the memory of the old one; life on Highland assumed its old sociability.

Frank set the precedent in my grandfather's studio, that arena of sequential filial frolicking that acquired a reputation over the years even it didn't deserve. Beer mugs and other symbols of adolescent glory had replaced J. P. Alley's pipes and photographs on the mantel. Frank held parties when he was home from college, attended by long-legged girls I fell in love with from a distance. Their laughter hung out in the darkness beyond the poplar tree, and sometimes a boisterousness that dismayed the neighbors. I don't know why my parents put up with this. I think the studio represented something quite different for each of them. Dad approved of partying in relative security; Mom liked sounds of life there. Occasionally she and Dad even took part, going out to be introduced to the right young people, many of whom were fond of them. Dan and I would hear my mother's laughter mix with the girls', and sometimes we couldn't distinguish one from the other.

Maybe I couldn't attend Memphis University School but I could run with some who did, or with those who went to East High, up the social ladder from Central. Frat boys wore robin's-egg-blue shirts with button-down collars, khakis with little buckles in the back, madras-covered belts, and loafers that held dimes; they progressed from Champale to sloe gin and 7-Up. The ones I looked up to were a couple of years older than I, replicas in some ways of my brother. A few took their preoccupation with money, violence, or sex beyond what was considered acceptable in Memphis, even though they were indisputably the right people.

11

HARLEY LAIRD'S ovoid, crew-cut head and thick shoulders seemed to fill the cockpit of his black MG when, after fraternity meetings, he would step over the car door and crank up that resonant little import. He didn't waste a lot of time beating pledges. Harley had things to do and the habit of scooping up people who engaged his imagination, grinning in a way that showed a lot of good Laird teeth. I had heard about Harley and another fraternity brother and friend of mine, T.J., traveling across town in the MG, in reverse, after Harley had been unable to get the car into forward gear. (He put the windshield down and sat on the hood, drinking beer while steering with his feet.) I had also heard that Harley's father was the second most important man in Tennessee.

The big silver Pontiac Harley drove to fraternity meetings on Sundays, when he wasn't driving the MG, carried a license plate bearing the single numeral 2, proof that his father answered only to the governor. Once Harley and his friends loaded cases of beer into the trunk at an ice house on Airways Boulevard and burned rubber without paying. I know this because I was in the car. A clerk got the license plate number and called the police; there had to be some mistake, the proprietor of the ice house was told by the state attorney general's office, after his call was bumped up, because the son of the second most important man in Tennessee wouldn't steal beer.

On another occasion the Pontiac's occupants threw bricks through a picture window on the edge of Galloway golf course owned by a man perceived by Harley to be a son of a bitch. And once Harley left me sitting in the dark parking lot outside the Pink Palace, Memphis's fusty old museum, while he climbed a drain pipe, opened a window he had unlatched during visiting hours, and stole a nineteenth-century dueling pistol.

At the wheel of the Pontiac, Harley once tried to force off a back road a Cadillac driven by a no doubt armed, middle-aged Memphian who had just left a north Mississippi gambling parlor — a failed attempt at highway robbery that leaves me, thinking about it after more than three decades, a little breathless. But the most enduring image is of Harley on his knees in the middle of a lawn in east Memphis, in summer, straddling another boy and swinging his big arms. The sound of Harley's fists against opposing flesh charges the darkness, while around him gambol dozens of spectators in Bermudas and Levi's, backlighted by the headlights of cars left at crazy angles in the street.

He favored knit shirts with little cloth alligators on them, because they showed off his breadth; his leisurely gait took up most of the pavement, but Harley's hands were surprisingly quick. A year older than I, he was everything an aspiring man should be: tough, daring, smart, funny, well connected, attractive to other men and to women for very different reasons, and ambitious in a naturally combative way. He played fullback for East High, offhandedly but well. His father sold something intangible but valuable — legal advice for men trying to beat Memphis's malleable zoning laws or to corner a commodity — when he wasn't telling the governor what to do, and he owned a big house across from Overton Park.

I played no major sports, and my father sold heating and air conditioning units. We lived in a house owned by my grandmother, in a neighborhood on the way to commercial oblivion, where a gift shop had opened next door. The big oaks on Highland hadn't been cut but the inexorable shift of the city cast even them in shadow. Money was a less obvious impediment than it might have been. I and boys and girls I knew operated according to what we considered our natural abilities, assuming ourselves to be at, or at least close to, the top of the social chain. In most cases we weren't even close, but we were made to feel like equal sharers in Memphis's postwar prosperity. So comfortably acquired and in many cases so new was the wealth that it sheltered for the moment even the children of distant aspirants. This familiar, seemingly graspable world of young, privileged white Memphis mirrored its adult counterpart, its compulsions played out in the street, in clubs, and on the lawns of those big houses in Chickasaw Gardens and along the western verge of the MCC golf course that still come imperceptibly together.

I thought the enormous discrepancies between my own life and that of someone like Harley Laird didn't really matter — a tribute also to my mother's insistence that we ranked — and believed that all would eventually be resolved in a gentle uplifting of people like me who found themselves without a mansion and a sports car. What brought Harley and me together I assumed was my God-given talent. At sixteen I weighed all of one hundred and twenty pounds but had fought outside the Rainbow Terrace Room while the Midnighters rollicked inside — maybe it was the El Dorados, the Drifters, or Frogman Henry. That and other encounters, flailings of fists, I survived by staying on my feet. I wasn't big but I was determined, and throwing a punch brought all the doubts and unspoken anxieties of my life into sudden, furious focus. A fight redefined you, even when you lost, and sometimes gloriously.

Harley engaged in real brawls and backed down ducktailed rogues in parking lots. My skirmishes demonstrated only that I was capable of the sort of explosive unreason that appealed to him. By that time something was clearly wrong with me; I knew it but couldn't have said what. I didn't really belong in either camp, rogues or the right people. The contradictions between the acclaimed godly mean, which supposedly fueled Memphis's phenomenal self-satisfaction, and what actually went on there were becoming apparent. I even suspected that belonging to Tau wasn't the most important thing that could happen to me. I had no special skills with which to replace the advantages of belonging, if I chose to give it up. By the end of the tenth grade my behavior suggested a profound inability to adapt to what was characterized as, and what I still believed to be, normal existence. I assumed I was stuck with the emerging version of myself, one that was belligerent, too daring, overly skeptical, unfocused, disdainful.

Harley seemed affected by none of this, at ease with himself and lacking all regrets, inhibitions, and worries. He was a person I knew I could never be, but even as an impossible model he remained a source of both excitement and self-esteem, if I could impress him. I knew that Harley was a "bad" person, not just physically violent but reckless in a basic way, as I wasn't, although I sought to emulate him.

I couldn't begin to keep up, and yet I tried. Together we challenged various notions of suitable behavior — what would become known as the System — and yet Harley managed to remain part of it, still puzzling to me. He got us into the kind of trouble I yearned for, proof of masculinity and significance beyond the daily platitudes in the mouths of adults and in the *Commercial Appeal.* I miss Harley in a way that has less to do with lost friendship than with heedless opportunity, a definition of adolescence that for many of the people I knew would not end until they died.

I see Harley now as a kind of mid-southern existentialist, before that word ever got to west Tennessee, a member of the elite whose behavior transcended the most egregious rogue's. On warm nights, after a date, he liked to go into a yard near his, wriggle through the open window of a car, and then with special tools, hanging upside down under the dash, his large feet protruding, extricate the radio. Harley didn't need the money, he enjoyed the risk. He threw a football game, missing a key tackle so the opposing team could win and he collect on a bet placed by a friend. The scam, not the money, provided the pleasure. He staged an illegal party in a rented roadhouse on the old Memphis-to-Nashville road and filled it with expectant teenagers who had paid for access to the half-dozen iced kegs. Only one had beer in it. As it was emptying, Harley strolled out to his MG and motored off, his pockets full of cash, a show of colossal sang-froid.

I don't remember many of our conversations. We talked about cars, football, beer, real and contrived cleavage, and what you did with a naked girl. My views on at least half those subjects were theoretical. "If she's stacked," Harley would say, "then don't go for her tits — that turns them off." Or, "You've got to keep their feet apart or they'll try to wiggle away." I was to watch out for the faked orgasm and to remember what was known as Harley's Theory, about the correspondence between the size of a girl's mouth and that other orifice.

I didn't know what to believe. Harley's appeal was the action he commanded, not the subtlety or even the truthfulness of his observations. I had other friends wittier and more capable of sarcasm — addicted to it, in fact — but none of them would dare Harley's instinctive, perilous acts. Mostly he and I talked about raising hell and exploits beyond the city limits. He wanted to fight for a cause and so, vaguely, did I, but not at the controls of an airplane, as Harley did. The romance of distant conflict played some part in the local ones, I think; spontaneous criminality was rationalized as preparation for a challenging, indefinite future. We imagined ourselves on opposite sides, for some reason, I among the ranks of some exotic nationality, preferably in a jungle, and Harley in the vanguard of power, doing his duty in a resplendent machine yet to be invented. The eerie thing is that, whereas my vision was vague and childish, Harley's was precise and would be precisely reflected in his manhood.

In the two years I ran around with him I never met his father. The subject rarely came up, and when it did Harley assumed uncharacteristic silence. He dropped by 491 South Highland occasionally, but his visits were brief; he clearly differed from my other friends, being older, bigger, less vulnerable. My father and mother didn't know what to make of him, only that he was wealthy and well connected, and wondered as they often did how I got to be chummy with someone so unexpected.

Harley's mother was the epitome of the right person, impeccably dressed even on weekdays, pleasant if unsmiling. She served mostly as a conduit for messages between Harley and his father. Harley's older sister had that flat, drawn gaze of southern debutantes who have seen more than enough of the behavior of the sort of men they must marry, and her comments on our activities and avowed plans were wickedly perceptive.

Girls generally fell into groups complicated by social standing but not ruled by it. To begin with, they were either chaste or unchaste. The former were the sort you would someday marry and whose designation you meanwhile halfheartedly sought to alter. Chastity tended toward the right side of the tracks, yet some of the most unchaste girls came from the right families. Curiously, a good girl's designation didn't necessarily change if she slept with someone she loved. Then she was a good girl touched with tragedy.

"Bad" was an imperfect concept when applied to girls, the word itself rarely used unless it pertained to those with names obviously — to us — sexual, like Fay or Yvonne. (You had to be really stupid to name your daughter Yvonne in Memphis.) They would make love to most anybody who came by to pick them up, and sometimes to two or three boys in succession, events I only heard about. Most girls who "did" were judged by the level of enthusiasm they brought to the act. Enthusiasm with more than one partner meant the girl was either bad or hopelessly sophisticated. Perceived variation in performance allowed each boy to think of himself as the best, the embodiment of valor or good looks that had at last fulfilled her expectations.

Years later, reading Peter Taylor's story "The Old Forest," set in Memphis, I realized that what had seemed to us a novel division was in fact standard operating procedure. We didn't refer to girls who did, or those who came from the wrong side of the tracks or the wrong side of the river and worked in thoroughly respectable jobs, as "demimondaines," wouldn't have known what the term meant, but we did treat them differently. Taylor's may have been an earlier generation, but the categorizing of girls according to current availability, connections, and future matrimony hadn't changed.

Veronica waded in dark water, holding up the hem of her skirt to reveal hefty but good legs that had not been shaved that day — a sign, I was sure, of rampant sexuality. It was Saturday. The brothers of Tau Delta Tau and their dates had gathered on the shore of Arkabutler, a reservoir in north Mississippi with a primordial vista: rotten stumps and a muddy littoral running to infinity. We boys lay on a patch of imported sand like shoats on a slow spit, drinking beer and practicing irreverence. Veronica was, I thought, underappreciated by her date, the lank, fastidious Rughead. Her smile lacked the hale camaraderie with which some girls kept boys at bay, and her brilliant blue eyes reflected depthless unconcern.

She was not petite but she was pretty, and had a reputation for warmth that bordered on the indiscriminate. She lived in a housing development between the big lawns of Walnut Grove and the attenuated commercialism of Summer Avenue, a transitional neighborhood, and unfortunately was a Baptist. But these facts lost significance when I talked to her later on the telephone; Veronica's natural breathiness affected my circulatory system in the same way a person would have by sitting on my chest.

We made a date. Her response to my tentative moves in the front seat of my father's pea-green, stick-shift Plymouth was immediate, passionate, and absolutely circumscribed by a vow she had made at a Baptist retreat to preserve her virginity until marriage. The interesting part was that Veronica provided such willing inspiration for undermining it. This led to more dates and discussion, and eventually to Sunday dinner with her parents, plump evangelists who prayed loudly over the meal, eyes clamped shut, but were otherwise tight-lipped. I knew the jokes about Baptists: a person transferring from a Baptist to a Methodist church automatically lowered the IQ averages of both. Baptists didn't copulate while standing up because somebody might think they were dancing. And so on. Veronica's mother asked me what church I belonged to, and I admitted, "St. John's."

Her father looked at me as if at a released felon. "I hear they're pretty liberal," he said.

They had been to service at least once that day. Veronica's churchgoing blouse didn't suit her large, light-absorbing breasts. Those, not God, were the center of the universe, obvious to Him and everyone else, a screaming unavoidability that hung over a tablecloth into which had been woven a rugged cross from which holy rays emanated. Veronica's obliging blue eyes stayed on her roast beef.

Her father asked, "All you fraternity boys wear those shirts with little buttons on the collars?"

"I guess so."

"What are they for?"

"For keeping your tie in, Daddy."

"Well, they must be hard to button."

Conversation turned to summer jobs. I had been working as a counselor at a summer camp north of Memphis, herding kids from the swimming pool to the archery range to the mess hall. Next year, I said, I hoped to be a lifeguard.

"Where?" asked Veronica's father. "At the kiddie pool?"

His wife, barely awake, doughy-looking, smiled noncommittally. Her husband made sounds like laughter. I had been told by the father of another girl, a midtown banker, "Try to be a good Christian and blend on in." Here was a dedicated Sunday school teacher who made his daughter go on retreats, and rather than proselytize her suitors, attacked them. I realized that some girls' fathers did indeed have a dim understanding of boyfriends' intentions, that some fathers weren't just automatons who provided couches and potato chips, but much worse.

"Veronica tells me," he said, "that your uncle's editor of the *Commercial*."

"Yes, sir."

"Well, why don't you get him off Bellevue Baptist's back?"

Later, as if dinner had never happened, Veronica and I made out in her living room, using the sound of the television set for cover, while her parents did whatever Baptists were supposed to do in their bedrooms on Sunday night.

She came by my house with other girls and boys. Mom said nothing about Veronica that I can remember — a rarity — and Dad averted his eyes from those preponderant parts of her that usually attracted so much indiscriminate male attention. Veronica tried to be demure there, too, but was basically unequipped for the role. Some girls just had too much too early of whatever it was that made them women — and not just breasts — and a natural, pleasant, essentially southern disposition that added to the suggestion of complaisance.

Mostly Veronica and I went to movies, and sometimes to parties that coalesced almost every night in the city, amidst banks of flowers and the herbaceous explosion of Memphis. Harley took up with a friend of Veronica's; we double-dated in the Pontiac belonging to the second most important man in Tennessee, eating barbecue at Willie King's drive-in and then catapulting over the viaduct, bound for Boyle's Lake. Harley already had a steady girl, who went to Miss Hutchinson's and who would be "coming out" in a year. By some mysterious circumlocution the subject of Harley's debutante never came up. I was learning by example rather than exegesis that some guys had two sorts of girlfriends, and that neither sort talked about the other.

The four of us would sometimes leave the Pontiac parked by the Toddle House and creep back to the studio, to test the elasticity of vows and to come to grips by increment with what was most definitely on our minds.

Sex, like the aura of hydrangea, hovered over everything that summer of 1957. Meanwhile Dad was looking for a new office and operating out of a cramped one down Highland Avenue, on the wrong side of the tracks. I worked there for a while, answering the telephone when he was away on calls, and taking orders. Commerce was a mystery to me. Someone I didn't know would call from a place I had never been to and ask for a piece of equipment I had never heard of. I would look up the serial number in a manual Dad had provided and then call up someone else I didn't know and read the number off. Somehow all this produced money.

The office had old, unfinished hardwood floors dark in the cracks. The place depressed me, depressed us both, I think. At that time big money was being made in Memphis in real estate, cars, banks, barges, soybeans, cotton, and Philippine mahogany. Sometimes Dad would take the bottle of Jim Beam out of the double desk drawer and tip it up. Although I was used to seeing this at home, it bothered me in the angled yellow sunlight and the inconsequence of a Memphis afternoon.

There, and sometimes in the car with my parents, on some local excursion of almost unbearable uselessness, I would look at Dad, so straightforwardly directed, and read into his unconscious movements — shifting gears, lighting a cigarette — a terrible, foregone obsolescence. He was all of forty-six, impossibly ancient in my view, bypassed, gone. I wondered what joy he could possibly find in life, why he bothered doing the things you did to stay alive, like brushing your teeth and putting on deodorant. I wondered why he didn't just say, one day, "To hell with you all," and take off. What was it about fathers that made them put up with their children and wives, and even try to like it? What had driven my father to forgive me after I took the car out when I wasn't supposed to and was rear-ended by a drunk society matron doing eighty, who sent me and my luscious date unharmed through an iron fence?

I couldn't wait to get home, out of the practical world and into the guise of prospective lover. I could think of little else. One Saturday, exposed to the world, I dragged the mattress out of the old servants' quarters, across the back yard, flattening the crabgrass, not even attempting to be surreptitious, and into the studio. The aspiring snow-job artist had given way to the no-quarter seducer. Someone — my parents, Dodo, Jack — must have noticed this remarkable preparation but said nothing, tacitly recognizing either an established ritual or the fact that I was no longer under control.

That night Veronica and I went to my grandfather's shrine by ourselves. An Ella Fitzgerald record of my brother's waited on the spindle; the mattress lay unavoidably in the middle of the floor. We knelt on it and started on the familiar progression, but Veronica knew that this time was different. I found a break in the fundamentalist front, and dove through; the physical disengagement of buttons and the clasp took a while, and then Veronica swung free in the almost-dark. Blouse and bra hanging, she gazed down at me and my tactile examination, and asked, "Why do you like to do that?"

Her Bermudas came off, so simple after so much speculation. They were followed by underpants, sturdy cotton charged with the power of what they had contained. Partially naked Veronica glowed; her skin felt cool, in sharp contrast to my own and to the night air. She lay down and waited patiently while I grappled with my own shorts. Then I took from beneath the mattress that emblem of maturity so familiar and yet difficult to put on, and in the course of a minute, maybe two, we traveled from nothingness into the kingdom of the knowing.

That an act thought about so intensely for so long could be done so quickly left us both dazed. Finally Veronica said, "I thought you were supposed to take off all your clothes."

"I don't guess you have to."

"Oh."

There was no other receptacle, so our protection ended up in my brother's college fraternity beer mug.

*

In the days that followed, Veronica seemed both distracted and repentant. I blamed myself for obliterating the old unconcerned, agreeable girl, and she blamed me, too. We broke up by telephone, got back together the same way, broke up again. We went to the studio one last time to make it final, and in the midst of that discussion Veronica lost both her blouse and her bra. This time even our socks went. I wasn't prepared, but what was launched couldn't be stopped. She moved beneath me with a surprising, unsorority-like assertiveness. What we were doing now bore little resemblance to what we had already done. In our mutual convulsion I glimpsed something astonishing and unfettered, and heard Veronica say, "What *happened?*"

For three weeks I lived in its shadow, the celebration of carnal joy so brief as to seem like a dream. I imagined myself dropping out of school and getting a job, leaving the house every morning like Dad and hitchhiking, not to Central, but to a filling station to pump gas, or maybe to Galloway golf course to caddie, to earn money, for what I wasn't sure. I couldn't imagine, as hard as I tried, being married to Veronica; I saw myself eating eternal Sunday dinner with her, her parents, and something in a high chair, smeared with jam. The sight of children's toys in passing cars filled me with low-grade panic. I couldn't talk about this with anyone, even Harley, who wouldn't get himself into such a dilemma, or if he had, would have shrugged off the consequences, whereas I got almost physically ill thinking of them.

Several times a day I telephoned Veronica and, though I vowed I wouldn't, asked, "Start yet?"

I had heard of boys knocking up girls and leaving the problem in their parents' hands. That wasn't an option with Veronica. Her father wouldn't allow an easy exit, and probably neither would mine. Dad's possible reaction inspired more morbid speculation. I wondered if he had ever been in this fix, and felt guilty about that, too, as if I were tainting him by association. For one brief, grotesque afternoon I saw the two of us as equals, stuck in the same vice. I resolved that if I ever got out of it I would turn my attention solely, religiously, to schoolwork, that I would labor unceasingly, like Ashley home from the Civil War in the movie version of *Gone With the Wind*, broken but radiant, replacing those rotten fence posts, the idea of sex banished.

Then Veronica called, and said, "I started."

12

I QUICKLY FORGOT my vow of celibacy. Veronica's and my affair became the envy of my friends, Harley included, but the relief of sexual tensions did not make me more pleasant or my life more productive, but the opposite. Thinking back, I am almost certain that Dad knew the truth about Veronica and felt powerless to affect my flooding testosterone. A standoff developed between us over other things, like grades and "attitude." Forbidden to leave the house, I left it anyway, by way of a rope ladder. Then, denied the use of the car, overcome with righteous resentment and still thinking myself tough, I came close to hitting Dad, or at least pretended to come close. This feint contained such Oedipal abandon that it frightened us both. After that, only work — necessary, unambiguous tasks — provided a medium of communication, and that edgy and sad.

Self-preservation persisted by the dumbest good luck. I waited to poleax a much bigger boy until Harley was present to drag him off me. I usually placed latex between me and Veronica. But luck could not prevent me from failing algebra and getting a D in Spanish. I was in the process of making the eleventh grade a waste and leaving myself with prospects closer to those of Humes and Tech High graduates than to the bright boys at Memphis University School, Central, and East.

Dad expected me to behave better and do better than he had behaved and done at my age, and so somehow affirm his worth; that I behaved and did worse meant my adulthood, if it ever arrived, would be even less certain than his and that our resentments would be common, double-edged. This situation had no winners and its effects bled into other lives like ink spilled onto an old sketch pad.

One spring night in 1958, Harley and I went together to the Rainbow Terrace Room for the Seven Sins Ball, Tau Delta Tau's annual money-raising extravaganza and indisputably a big deal. Seven beautiful girls, chosen by ballot from the ranks of the sororities to represent the Sins, appeared on stage, bumping and grinding in low-cut, body-sucking silk, while Jerry Lee Lewis or someone like him perched like a monkey on a white piano, banging out rock 'n' roll that frats and rogues alike had paid to absorb and so briefly lived more or less in harmony. Because Sun Records brought bands to Memphis for recording sessions, we were able to hire those same bands cheaply, if we threw in a bottle of bourbon for each musician. We drank Harley's version of the Tom Collins — it was made with cheap rum and Thunderbird — and the two of us ended the night in the potting shed behind the big house belonging to Memphis's most successful hardwood importer, smashing empty flowerpots over each other's heads and laughing maniacally.

The next morning I discovered that my teeth had grown fur and the backs of my eyeballs had acquired a fiery glaze. I vaguely remembered seeing my father in his boxer shorts, in the back yard, hands on hips, surveying the calamity of my homecoming. I didn't remember driving the Plymouth through the fence but I did know something unfortunate had occurred.

Standing over me, staring, was our maid, Dolly, a wild-looking woman known for irreverence. She said, "You smell like cat piss."

When she was gone I got out of bed and felt my way along the hall of the attic (long since converted to bedrooms by Dad), marveling at an erection that defied my general misery. It flatly refused to point anywhere but upward. The only alternative to relieving myself against the ceiling of the bathroom was standing on my head, a thought that threatened me with nausea. Slowly, deliberately, I rose on the tips of my toes, put my hands on the wall, and inclined my body so as to gradually menace the enamel target.

I was wanted on the telephone.

"Jim?" It was the voice of Laurel Moore. "You ready?"

"I'm sick," I said.

"Jee-um!"

An hour later I sat in a low, slatted chair on the front porch, wearing a white button-down shirt and a tie upon which swam paisleys like mutant spermatozoa. My khakis had been pressed and the little buckle in the back reassembled. My madras jacket lay on the swing, a swatch of utter tastefulness. My white bucks had been dusted with the puff that came in the maintenance kit and then stomped clean of the incriminating evidence of preparation, a task that had to be interrupted in order to drink another tumbler of water and take an Alka-Seltzer.

My chair, set at an angle to the street, offered a view of Jack reading a paperback novel with his usual absorption, halfheartedly rocking. It was the same Jack I had been seeing for seventeen years, but that day he looked different, his hair and dentures enhanced in the burning light of remnant alcohol. I sensed doom abroad in the world of the hung-over and expiring, in the face of my responsibility: I had accepted, the night before, a last-minute request to escort Laurel, maid to the Queen of Delphi, to a Cotton Carnival luncheon at the Peabody Hotel. She had been stood up, and I was her only prospect.

Laurel was a friend only, a Miss Hutchinson's product whose social standing and current demand on me had put off my atonement for the destroyed fence. She appeared in a chrome-streaked convertible creeping through the glare of noon, a Chrysler with swept-back tail fins driven by one of a score of boys chosen each spring to chauffeur Cotton Carnival royalty to the all-important events. I slipped on sunglasses, picked up my jacket, and crossed the lawn, already sweating. The good-natured Laurel watched me with misgiving. Her well-brushed, chablis-colored hair was secured under a scarf; she wore nothing between her large, frank eyes and the elements. Like many of her friends, she seemed genetically impervious to the sun.

We sped along Central Avenue, horn blaring. No policeman would stop us: Cotton Carnival royalty was expected to speed. Sometimes motorcycle cops took up the lead out of respect, lights flashing, sirens whooping. The pleasure I should have felt sitting in the back seat of a new convertible with a beautiful girl was offset by the need to concentrate on the horizon, beyond the misshapen right ear of our driver, another Central High junior. Laurel patted my hand with her own cool, dry one, slightly roughened by regular contact with the handle of a tennis racket.

We disembarked at the Second Street entrance to the Peabody. Inside, I said, "I have to go to the bathroom," and started down the stairs. The hotel had been around for a hundred years, I assumed. I knew the story of the Confederate general riding his horse into some lobby — actually it was the

Hotel Gayoso — when the city was occupied by Union forces and escaping into Mississippi, proving how daring and brave were the Confederate officers. The story also proved that outrageous things happened in hotels. Nobody would get upset if a person happened to calmly vomit there.

In the men's room I crossed reflecting white tiles to a stall with marble sides and threw up with precision through the hole in a wooden toilet seat polished by the posteriors of generations of Memphians. The black attendant turned on the cold-water tap in a washbasin. The epaulets on his uniform were tattered; he looked at me with what I thought was great solemnity while I doused my face with water. I felt a towel pressed into my hand. "You want a Alka-Seltzer?" I accepted, and gave him whatever change I had.

I found Laurel on the mezzanine, outside the Venetian Room. It was full of people my parents' age. The wretchedness of my condition had an inverse effect upon perception: everything seemed larger, brighter, stranger. Big crystal chandeliers dangled over tables where beaded tumblers of water perspired into the starched white cloths. A man in gray seersucker came toward us with short, mincing steps. Bunched flesh obscured his eyes and overflowed a collar buttoned down over a striped tie. He said, "Laurel, my dear, it's so nice to see you," in a Delta drawl that pushed the words out like half-baked biscuits. *Lal, mah deah, izzo niza see ya.*

He hugged her with a little too much enthusiasm, and asked, "How's your father?" *Ha's yo fah-thah?*

I was in the presence of royalty. The King of Delphi turned to me and asked, "And who's this fine young man?" *An' hooz thiz fi-un yun may-un?*

"This is Jim Conaway."

The King's first name was Bev, the truncated version of a Mississippi ancestor's last name and a sure sign of lineage. I knew several boys with last names for first ones: Lamar,

Carruthers, Cash. Bev suggested a drink. I ordered a gin and tonic — I had heard about hair of the dog — and saw Laurel's mouth open. But Cotton Carnival meant free booze when you were underage, with the acquiescence of adults; you didn't pass up that chance. I felt a cool tendril of effervescence from throat to solar plexus and decided that everything was going to be all right.

Laurel and I took our seats at the head table, where pats of butter emblazoned with the Peabody crest floated in ice water; the burnished silver dish had been heaped with mayonnaise. There is the claim that southerners behave peculiarly because they all suffer from mayonnaise poisoning, but I ate only tomato aspic, to have something to do while the King began his speech. I don't remember the words, only the assertion that Memphis sat at the end of one great decade — the fifties — and on the threshold of another, a time of tranquility during which some people would make a lot of money. During the sixties, the King added, Memphis would remain the largest inland hardwood market in the nation. *Tha lah-jist hodwood mah-ket ina nayshun.*

I realized too late that I was in trouble again and that the door leading to the mezzanine could not be reached. I pushed back from the table and stood up. Exposure to a crowd was scary in any circumstances, but this went beyond the bounds of awfulness. I was about to commit an act that would disgrace not only Laurel and myself but everyone I knew, and possibly the entire city. I would never be invited to anything again and neither would any of my relatives. This would be the last thing to go down on my permanent record.

I saw, behind the podium, a small door cut into the elaborate molding. With feigned casualness I strolled past the King of Delphi, opened the door, stepped into a small room full of stacked chairs, carefully closed the door behind me, and exploded.

When I emerged, the King was saying, "We have no labor problems. Our people are accustomed to work. They know how to work. They *wah-unt* to work . . ." I sat back down. Laurel pretended nothing had happened, but I could see a lot of the whites of her eyes.

We left after the applause. In the lobby I told her I had to go to the men's room again. There I passed the same mournful black face and plunged into the same cubicle to perform the same function. The attendant again ran water into the basin, where I washed my face and took a towel, and yet another Alka-Seltzer.

Because we were leaving a Cotton Carnival event rather than going to one, the driver was mercifully prevented from speeding and blowing the horn. We crossed Parkway and shot up onto the overpass that linked us with Poplar Avenue. Laurel, who lived far to the east, asked, "Want to come home with me for a while?"

She held my hand. After the driver had peeled out of the Moores' driveway, leaving us at the edge of a big, freshly cut lawn, I turned and threw up into the vetch.

"Jim, how many times have you done that?"

"Four."

"I think you ought to call the doctor."

Inside, I dialed the number of our family physician, a leonine man with a mustache, a rare commodity in Memphis that was said to make women eager to be examined by him. I told him my symptoms, and he said, "Stop taking Alka-Seltzer!"

Laurel sat in the cool, aqueous glow of her living room, my head in her lap. I gazed upward, past her breasts, at the smooth confluence of neck and chin, wishing for a girlfriend with her possibilities and for a capacity within myself to handle her, if I ever found one.

*

Late afternoon sunlight cut through the poplar tree in our back yard, full of caterpillar webs and ragged, lime-green leaves. The back of the house, struck by the hard, angled shadow of the garage where the Plymouth rested serenely, had closed its eyes to the sun; somewhere on the other side of the drawn shades sat Mom, Dodo, Jack, and Dan, all aware of the transaction taking place outside. I stood close to Dad in his fresh white T-shirt, faded khakis, and knit belt with the silver Seabees buckle. He looked youthful, assigned to some military action enjoyed not for the violence but for the problems it posed. This problem was a broken fence, and as he surveyed it he reconstructed the course of events that had led up to the parting of the post at ground level.

"Moisture," he said. "We didn't coat it high enough with creosote." Creosote was one of Dad's favorite substances. "Look how the grain deteriorated unevenly."

As an engineer, although a degreeless one, he saw the world as a congeries of physical forces in constant strife. The way to prevail was to understand and arrange them so that nature could be deflected, so structures and people could rise up and stay put instead of falling down, as they were constantly trying to do. The night before I had assisted gravity, a fact Dad was willing to forgive simply because I had missed the posts holding up the chinning bar, which would have dented the Plymouth's fender, and because I had gone to bed without an argument.

"You passed within an inch and a half of it," he said. "You weren't going fast, just steady. When you took the fence out, the car stalled. I heard you start the engine again."

I picked up the spade and began to dig at the interred bit of post. Dad appraised this course of action and signaled approval by not telling me to stop. The smooth handle bent and the blade came up with black earth that in the course of my lifetime had supported weeds, flowers, and the grapevine on its wooden trellis. Dad thrust the crowbar into the rotten post and, using the broken end as a fulcrum, brought pressure to bear. Veins stood out in arms that, like mine, were knotty, but better developed. The post moved. He got more of a bite with the crowbar, and out came the offender.

This left a hole for the new post, a too easy solution. He picked up the post-hole digger and assaulted the bottom of the hole, driving the elliptical blades with heaving down strokes, tweezing out the dirt. He said, "That ought to do it."

He upended the new post into the renovated hole. It sank to the line of applied creosote. Dad clamped the level against it to assure absolute verticality. After unlimbering the tape measure, he checked the distance from ground to the bottom of the lowest rail on the surviving fence. Using a try square he marked off a line on the new post with a pencil with special flat lead.

I snugged the board on the pencil line and Dad drove new nails with hammer blows that rang in my head. We repeated the process for the middle rail. That left only the top one. Dad could have measured the plank against the fence but instead applied the tape, square, and pencil, then carried the board to the picnic table. "Would you like to bring me that saw?"

The handle was inlaid with the manufacturer's brass nameplate, worn smooth. The white ash showed through the stain. Sawing was the real test of carpentry. Again, "Pulling's as important as pushing." Dad's edges were perfectly square; the vibrant saw would never bind in his hand. He finished with a deft half-stroke that left no splintered wood, and fit the board like a puzzle piece, post to post.

I drove the nails while Dad kneed it, keeping it upright, plumb. "All it needs is paint," he said, and my exhaustion must have been palpable. "We'll do that later" — words that always meant freedom, this time to sleep.

13

THAT SUMMER I worked as a lifeguard at the Memphis Country Club, a plum of a job that I owed to my aunt. It allowed me to make extra money teaching kids to swim and provided as many chocolate malts and club sandwiches as I wanted, prepared by a Negro woman behind the counter, Doris, who put up with contending demands of a dozen ravenous members at once. Those eating out under the umbrellas were served by young Negro men not much older than I, polite, harried, sweat running down into the collars of their white jackets. The quavering, blue-green rectangle of water nearby, focus of everyone's waking dream, heat dissipater, detoxifier, courtship arena for three generations, and aquatic playpen, was my responsibility and that of another lifeguard named Mason, who perched in the chair, bronzed biceps lapping the armrests, daring people to drown.

Because I was attending summer school in the mornings, I couldn't open up the pool and so had to work into the night. On odd days I cleaned the filters in the humming shadows of a pump room that smelled of chlorine and seepage; many times, after I turned out the lights and went down to the locker room to dress, I came up again to a faint, illicit plashing and saw dark forms creeping away — black boys from Orange Mound, sneaking a swim.

By July, my body had mahoganized everywhere except an albino strip of midriff. I wore a canvas cap with a round brim and a whistle on braided plastic, used to pierce the misbehavior of ten-year-olds. I gazed occasionally into the corners of the pool, in case bodies cramped on cheeseburgers or gin had lodged there, and then went back to my favorite pastime, my new dalliance. More than once, in the midst of a particularly inept act by Holden Caulfield, or some tragically offhand comment by Nick Barnes, I would hear soft but censorious tones and look down into matronly sunglasses. "Ma'am?" I would say, and the woman standing there, shifting from one foot to the other, would answer with some variation of "How in the world are you gonna save my little boy with your nose in that *book?*"

Something had happened between the Seven Sins Ball and the beginning of summer: literature. My brother was in part responsible for this. Just out of college, Frank had pushed several books on me, one including a poem, "The Waste Land," written by a guy who had a problem with Episcopalianism. I couldn't understand the poem but recognized in all those classical allusions and other obscurities an alternative to the reigning perspectives. The narrator seemed uncertain about life, which was a comfort, like the realization that most of those around me couldn't have understood "The Waste Land" either.

So were the Beats responsible for this remarkable surge of intellectual interest. Those distant, nonconformist voices were barely audible in Memphis in 1958. What became a local beatnik cell was not a tribute to the force of the movement in the United States, or proof of our perceptiveness or artistic daring. It was just another form of rebellion, and an effective one.

Three years earlier, Allen Ginsberg had read "Howl" aloud at the City Lights Bookshop in San Francisco. *On the Road* was a best seller the year before, and *The Evergreen Review* burned with literary insurrection against the civilization of Dwight Eisenhower and Norman Vincent Peale. We in Memphis couldn't claim to have suffered from the most celebrated traumas of the fifties, McCarthyism and the Bomb, neither of which was expected in Memphis, even though the Russians would no doubt have loved to flatten the home of Cotton Carnival. But there was a strong bias against anyone who behaved or spoke in a way not considered "normal" in Memphis. Talk of Communists in local government was too far-fetched, but not an open detestation of things un-American, which essentially meant un-Memphian.

Race was somehow part of it. Any questioning of accepted roles and objectives could bring surprisingly nasty retorts from my parents' friends and relatives; I saw those same expressions on the faces of men who had gotten out of their cars during our ROTC parades around Central High and leaned on their hoods to watch with grim satisfaction as we sweated in scratchy uniforms, holding our M-1s. Adults talked seriously of "them" having too much influence, not necessarily Communists or Negroes but a vaguer, more inclusive collection of doubters, unappreciators, and those "out of step" who lived elsewhere and might try to impose their collective will on the cleanest and quietest city in America.

I had failed Spanish and so had to hitchhike to Tech every morning to make it up. There, rogues in T-shirts and unbelted Levi's hanging in miraculous mid-pelvic suspension, probable dyslexics, borderline retards, and assorted pimply screw-ups all suffered under Miss Thatcher, who wore clownish rouge and had an aversion to touching. She opened the door with a tissue, dusted off the desk and chair with same, even used tissue to grip chalk and eraser. Being lumped with the academically halt in the sweltering room awakened me to the awfulness of my situation.

After class I would make my way to Poplar Avenue, careful not to stare at the drivers of the curbside custom jobs, and catch the bus. I would read while passing through Dad's old neighborhood — the greasy spoon Henry's Lunch, the cavernous windows of St. Peter's orphanage, the patchy greens of Overton Park golf course we both had putted on as fourteen-year-olds — barely aware of it. Past car dealerships, Willie King's, the viaduct above the web of railroad tracks, and the ongoing contention between residences and businesses on the city's unrolling, horizonless plain.

Novels revealed a tumult of emotion and missteps I had thought were mine alone. Faulkner wrote unsparingly about people who must have been kin to me; I sat in his prose like a biscuit in pan gravy, and then one morning *The Sound and the Fury* began to make at least a little sense and I felt triumphant. With Hemingway, I was alive to exotic Parisian highballs and people who spoke another language that somehow was still English. Curiously, Dostoyevsky and Turgenev seemed more pertinent to life in Memphis than Hemingway or Faulkner. I had barely squeaked through chemistry that year with a C minus, having read *Crime and Punishment* propped inside my chemistry text. Now, walking across Chickasaw Gardens to the pool in the late morning heat, I found that shady precinct heavy with literary association: the house of the current Queen of Tau was a *dacha,* the MCC golf course beyond it a southern steppe populated by men in plaid Bermudas.

Reading was indisputably connected to "outside influences" and therefore more alarming to adults than drinking too much or driving too fast. That was a great satisfaction to me. It had a social component as well. My older brother and his friends, including girls, talked about books. A beard, symbol of what was wrong with books, showed up on the face of Fred, the son of the owner of a record store. He listened to Dave Brubeck and other practitioners of "contemporary" jazz, using a new high-fidelity record player. What Fred played were not records, but "albums." They had to be handled a certain way that left no fingerprints to interfere with the sound. To properly appreciate this music, you had to position yourself precisely in a room.

I was most impressed that Fred willingly exposed his beard to the jaw-dangling hostility of his neighbors, something I wouldn't have been brave enough to do even if I could have grown one. Frank grew a beard and was promptly fired from his lifeguarding job at the University Club. Memphis's best clubs affected British managers — I had to deal with one at the MCC — and the University Club manager told my brother, "I thought homosexuals and beards went together."

Frank said, "That's funny. I thought it was homosexuals and British accents."

The exchange delighted my father when he heard about it, although he didn't like Frank's beard either. Dad's general response to budding Memphis bohemianism was interesting in that he altered none of his views and ridiculed much of what passed for culture, yet he held on to his popularity among my brother's friends. Dad equated novels with "adult comic books" and, after Fred received a draft deferment as a conscientious objector, announced, "Fred just lost his last chance to be a man."

Dad must have seen me as another potential casualty to literature, when what he wanted for a son was an engineer. I think he was in some way thankful that I was at least interested in something. My own friends with full-blown intellectual pretensions treated Dad as a kind of anthropological treasure, the unabashed American male, biased but friendly, unafraid to say what was on his mind. Mostly Taus, they included a drummer named Joe; Rughead, who had decided to be an artist; and Jack Kelly of the ubiquitous pipe. Bobby Metcalf, the most exhaustive reader among us, mapped the distant courses of Ferlinghetti, Corso, and other writers we otherwise would never have heard of. Their fathers' authority was so easily devalued in our eyes. One poor man spent a part of each day sitting on a therapeutic spike to ease his hemorrhoids, a fact that relegated him to absurdity in all matters; another was forever discredited because his wife drank too much and had to be extricated from the rosebushes by her maid.

Mom was generally more receptive to our new pose than Dad, and somewhat entitled, as a painter herself. Suddenly art was more than museum fare and make-work for Memphis's various women's clubs. Art was cool. Mom had been painting most of her life, keeping in practice with correspondence courses and the occasional trip to Alison's Wells, an art colony in north Mississippi. Dad went along on those excursions, drinking beer and trying to talk to landscape painters and watercolorists about something he knew nothing about and secretly considered trivial. The idea that my mother had a bona fide claim on the new aesthetic bothered me. I wanted parental absence from the big questions, not participation. Where before I had rejected authority, I now saw myself above it, irritated by the fact that Dad even knew who Faulkner was and that Mom had heard of Picasso.

I didn't share my thoughts with my parents, for different reasons. My father's reaction to most developments was predictable. My mother saw more possibility in life but she seemed unreliable to me, in thrall to "proper" opinions put forward no doubt to moderate what she saw as my extreme behavior. Temperamentally I was closer to her than to Dad, which was part of the problem. Wary of her emotional excesses, recognizing myself there, I put up a fence between us that came down only when we argued, and then resoundingly. The existence of girls made things worse. She was female, too, and so couldn't be thought about too much. She knew the "wrong sort" of girl when she saw one, and this made me uncomfortable, although not uncomfortable enough to stop taking them out. The right sort of female, in my mother's view, was a lot like her. I was leery of mock southern solicitousness that, after several years' practice, became second nature to some girls when they dealt with boys, and most everything else. In its worst manifestations this spun all ideas and impulses in cotton candy. My mother was not like that, although she was quite capable of the deception; sometimes it was hard to tell guise from reality. I found emotional equilibrium, self-sufficiency, and strong, contrary opinions in girls sexy, as long as these qualities coincided in a conventionally pleasing package.

By now Harley occupied another universe. He had graduated from high school and was bound for Annapolis in September and eventually, he hoped, for a war. His behavior, if anything, had gotten wilder. That summer he and friends went on a rampage during which they threw beer bottles into a firehouse. When they were finally apprehended by police, one of the boys was wearing around his neck a toilet seat wrenched from the men's room of Dobbs' Steak House. Nothing happened to them, of course. Other antics included hanging out of an open convertible as it raced down Poplar and bowling with stolen balls into three lanes of oncoming traffic.

I was no longer up to all that, and Harley knew it. His final act as a member of Tau Delta Tau had been a political campaign to get me elected president, his tactics akin to those of Boss Crump. Lobbying in a member's living room had put me over the top when I didn't even want to be president, was losing interest in fraternities, wasn't sure I could handle the job, and had misgivings about the probable views of Hemingway and Faulkner on the subjects of ritual and the rolling of pledges in elephant dung.

The old spontaneous accord was gone. I both regretted and welcomed the loss. Harley's view of literature was closer to my father's than to mine; his attempts to sound authoritative on the subject — and Harley never lacked for authority — embarrassed us both. One night, at the wheel of the Pontiac, he turned, smiled ruefully, and said, "You know, Con, I can tell you're gonna be one of those 'contemporary' bastards."

Veronica, too, had no line to the new, bookish reality. A breakup was inevitable, but not the sort that occurred. Teenage inadvertence was unsuited to what had become a thoroughly adult passion, and yet I almost casually admitted to her that I had "slept" with another girl, a former conquest of Harley's who came out of her house after I threw gravel at her window, and crawled into the back seat of her father's car. This bit of cruelty on my part — half confession, half boast — left Veronica speechless, a sloppy climax that would come back to me.

The girl in question was a year older than I and already in the college mode, gone in mind from Memphis; she is the dark element in that hot, transitional summer. At closing time she would drop by the MCC pool and wait. When everyone else was gone we would descend to the pump room and lie on a chaise dragged down specifically for that purpose. Serenaded by throbbing machinery, cooled by dank concrete, not bothering with protestations of affection, we made love determinedly and afterward lay panting in the subterranean darkness. Sometimes we would emerge to see, strung out along the edge of the golf course, the dark silhouettes of the illicit swimmers, clothes bundled under their arms.

*

This girl had nothing in common with members' daughters with names like Hutty, Doony, even Poopsy. In tennis whites, they elegantly displayed the basics of the game on MCC's emerald courts. Most said things like "Who's that *cree-chuh?"* when referring to some boy in a passing convertible, but a few had brains as well as accomplished backhands. In the evenings they might pass through the club, bound for the Whirlaway, out on Airways Boulevard, where beer was served without much regard for IDs and where, after work, I could dance with those same girls I had protected from drowning during the day. The songs "Summer Place" and "It's All in the Game" outshone anything Dave Brubeck could possibly have come up with, the lyrics assuming a sentimental power beyond the reach of any novel, beyond even sex, accompanied by the feel of sheer cotton over firm, suntanned, mostly innocent backs.

One girl had dark hair framing an oval face, with lashes spreading laterally at the edges, and the impeccable timing of a small person who was "sharp." Her words unsettled boys weighing twice as much as she, but mostly it was her pauses and the way she looked at you. Kittridge Smith's father owned a transport company in south Memphis and had raised up in the eastern part of the city a palatial, vaguely French façade through which passed the rightest of the right young people. That Kit attended Miss Hutchinson's was axiomatic. That she and I fell into a rivalry over who had read the most books was fortuitous and unlikely.

Kit and some other Hutchinson's girls my age were too sophisticated for most high school boys and so went out with older ones, including my brother and his friends. They came to Frank's parties in the studio, which rang now with the Modern Jazz Quartet and *Bolero.* I came, too. It seemed that everybody in Memphis wanted to be a writer — a sure sign was the wearing of Bermudas without socks — and Kit had specific views on this and most things, from Kahlil Gibran to

Harley Laird. (The former was interesting but limited, she said, and the latter a menace.) I remember her unsolicited view of my friend Rughead, the aspiring artist: "Maybe he can draw, but he doesn't have *it*."

I didn't know what *it* was, but wasn't about to reveal this. I was amazed that Kit could match the young men around us when it came to arguing. She remained uncommitted to any of them, as far as I could tell, including an ardent older cousin of mine and a dispossessed Arkansas scion named Bink who had been to Spain, an enormous advantage. Bink was one of those southerners with a hamlet named after his family, an expanse of cotton and beans with a few shacks of that luminous gray that seemed to come with rural poverty, and a lake full of stumps and lily pads. His family had more money than I could imagine, in a trust fund controlled by men who would not give Bink enough of it. My mother thought a lot of him and asked Bink to "try to get through to Jim," meaning set me on the right path, as if Bink could recognize it. His method of doing this was to drink beer out of big, beaded pitchers in Gino's tavern, and talk. There we discovered that we were both in Kit's orbit.

Her older sister wanted to be an actress and her mother had been one. Among the many people coming to the Smiths' were a theatrical producer with vague ties to Hollywood and a florid man who had made money in advertising in Memphis but evinced a sophistication at odds with the place. For Kit's birthday he gave her a framed Klee print that everyone praised. It reminded me of a balloon with eyes, but I praised it, too. Both men were probably in love with her blond older sister, but no open courtship was ever apparent at the Smiths'. This was one of many things I couldn't understand. Another was the way Mr. Smith treated me, not simply offering gin and tonics or, when the weather turned, scotch and sodas, but joking the way men did among themselves, assuming common ground when none existed, making me feel a part of something worldly and alive.

Here was a house that did not seem captive to finances, where conversation turned on issues beyond Memphis's social and political confines — on New York drama, Ivy League colleges, Europe. People of various ages lived what seemed like an ongoing, erudite party, Mrs. Smith interrupting her serving of hors d'oeuvres to recast herself in old roles of Ophelia or Candida ("'his industry for my livelihood! his dignity for my position!'"), Kit saying "Mother" in her subdued but emphatic way, her big sister laughing tipsily, and Mr. Smith providing good humor as willingly as he provided space, liquor, food, and probably cash to all those requesting it.

The closest I saw him to anger was early one morning when he walked out the doorway leading to the car port, on his way to play golf, and discovered Kit and me sitting on the step, deep in a conversation that had begun around midnight. "You're up early," he said, a firmness about his jaw. I can still see him driving off to the country club, head erect, mouth open in song.

Kit's and my talks could string a whole week together. Full of pauses, profundities, clashes, they surprised us both by their tenacity. "How do *you* know what 'iconoclastic' means?" Kit asked, exasperated by the discovery. I had come across the word somewhere; it was pure luck. Kit would counter with a reference to a writer I hadn't heard of. She would serve me thin strips of raw steak cut on the board in her kitchen and laved with Durkee dressing, an impossible sophistication. She would play Odetta on the stereo: "Heave her up and away we'll go, Way up in Cal-i-forn-ee-ooo."

In a way we were no better suited to each other than Harley and I had been. She intended to apply to a prestigious women's college in New England; my prospects seemed limited to the University of Tennessee in Knoxville, and not even that if I couldn't graduate. There was the occasional admission, indirectly, of affection, but a wariness remained, a realization that she was a virgin and I wasn't and that this distinction, as well as other important things, was freighted with a future I hadn't thought much about.

My brother's last party of the summer sprawled out of doors. I, surrogate host, uncertain of Kit's interest in me, inadvertently went to sleep on the grass in the middle of a discussion with her. I woke up before dawn to the miraculous sight of Kit Smith still sitting there, holding my hand.

Later, I was told by Bink, "All she talks about is Jee-um, Jee-um, Jee-um . . ."

14

THE GRAY stone house in Overton Park where Dad had grown up had been sold years before. My great-uncle Yank, who had never found a replacement for his opera singer, refused to leave the neighborhood. He rented various rooms in the upstairs of houses much like it; he took my brother Dan to the Mid-South Fair, but then his money began to run out and his mind to wander.

On Sundays, someone would drive to midtown from east Memphis to fetch Yank, and find him partially shaved and incompletely dressed. His clothes — all those dark suits — lay in piles on the floor, his round-brimmed black hat cast onto a chair. In the midst of the disorder stood the photograph of Yank's singer.

While being driven back to Overton Park after Sunday dinner, Yank would say to me, "You're sure going fast," when I wasn't, or "You don't seem to have any trouble seeing at night," when the sun had barely set.

My mother used Yank as an example of what my father should avoid becoming, although she meant no cruelty and never said anything in front of Yank. But when Dad displayed too much of his habitual authority, or refused to listen, she would say, "You're wrong about that," words Yank had used. They brought Dad up short every time.

Yank came to live with us on Highland Avenue for a while, another tension in a house already under generational stress, stuffed now with the prospect of aging. Jack had become an old, if still hale, man; Dodo had assumed round shoulders. Most of their money was gone, much of it given to relatives, including my family. There would be another summer or two in Bucks County, and another visit to St. Petersburg, but not in the style to which they had once been accustomed and not with the same anticipation.

Yank was moved into the room in the back of our house where Frank and I had lived before moving upstairs. In the late afternoons he would stand in the hall, his watery blue gaze on a scene we couldn't share. This happened more than once when I had a friend in the house, an embarrassment I couldn't apologize for without making it worse. Although never diagnosed, Yank's problem was obviously dementia. Most things depressed me then, but Yank did particularly; he had once seemed invulnerable, bound to win any ruckus, unperturbed by a world that was understandable and containable. Sometimes he would make it out to the porch, drawn by the sound of music — now classical — on the record player, and stand contemplating a landscape he didn't recognize and was too reticent to comment upon.

He ended up in that same nursing home on Poplar Avenue, a gruesome irony. Toward the end they put him in a crib with a net over it, not something I was supposed to see. Dad apologized for the fact that I did see it, and I felt sorry for him — almost the degree of sorrow I felt for Yank. Dad had paid so much of the costs of that place, first for Mamie, then for his mother, then for Yank. He blamed Yank's lonely demise on his bachelorhood, as if Yank should have exchanged one woman for another. But what Dad saw there haunted him, as it haunts me.

There were bright spots that last year of high school. Frank was a graduate student, self-sustaining, and my parents again began looking for a house of their own. I, in a reversal unexpected by everyone, began to study and to make good grades. Kit and her sister had awakened me to the importance of college as a conduit to the great beyond, even as Kit contended with me on everything from vocabulary to French symbolist poets, just one thing I pretended to know something about.

At the Smiths' I met boys a bit older but no smarter than I, home from eastern schools. They shared an aspiration I couldn't quite grasp and an assurance I marveled at. It was at the Smiths' that fall that I saw garters on men for the first time, revealed as these Ivy Leaguers sat with their legs crossed, drinking Mr. Smith's scotch. They talked about places I had read about in Salinger and Fitzgerald, where people rode trains and skied and found themselves in dark-paneled bars with beautiful young women who went to similar schools.

In direct opposition to my hankering for literature was leftover high school frat-ism. Having been elected president of Tau by Harley, I was bound to officiate at the weekly meetings, not a comfortable position for a beatnik sympathizer. Buckles on my trousers were of no interest now, but I had to wear them, and to pretend to care who pledged, and whether or not Tau hired the El Dorados or the Redtops for the next Seven Sins Ball. I couldn't wait to get home and put on rubber thongs and walk around thinking about poetry. I imagined myself, strolling on the MCC golf course at dusk, stumbling upon a beautiful, lithe poetess, unsuspected all these years, knowing that Memphis harbored no such person and that Kit was as close as I would come.

Toward the end of the year I abdicated my presidential

authority to the vice president, who was eager for it. Kit chided me. "You're shirking responsibility," she said, and my parents adored her for this and for her solicitousness, not just a southern girl's good manners but genuine affection. I was more or less irrelevant to their relationship, which I found extremely annoying — it was humiliating to be jealous of your own parents. Kit's admonitions to improve myself made romantic advances tricky, too. She was amenable up to a point, but, kissing her, I felt an intimacy that had as much to do with knowledge as with sex. I thought she saw into a part of me I had managed to keep hidden from others, full of self-doubt and emotional extremes, and this unsettled me. Sometimes the simple fact of me seemed to scare her.

In the way she held and then stopped me, in the dark corners of her restraint, I sensed a larger reservation. I felt as if I had invented the urges that drove us off the narrow intellectual path and — inconclusively — onto the brocade couch in her sitting room.

Some nights we took part in Memphis's unofficial literary salon, an extraordinary phenomenon in a house on Jefferson Avenue, in a seedy midtown neighborhood hedged by gas stations and appliance stores. The windows were covered with white doilies; the door was opened by a formal old woman who sent us up a switchback stairway lined with photographs of vaguely familiar people looking like geniuses, framed poems constructed of words and pictures cut out of magazines, and arrowhead and gem collections. Standing at the top, almost as wide as he was tall, wearer of a pencil-thin mustache, was the closest thing Memphis had to a poet laureate. His name was Kenneth Beaudoin, and he would say, "Children, *do* come up."

He had lived in Greenwich Village in its heady years, a near-mythic association. We thought of famous writers and artists as faces in aspic, not as people one knew; he spoke of them as friends, remarkably calm in recollection. He worked at night as a dispatcher for the Memphis Police Department and wore flower-print shirts and rubber thongs when he did it — odd, gutsy behavior in a city known for abusive cops and the common brand of homophobia, one that most of his male "children" shared. Beaudoin's apparent equilibrium in a society that despised much of what he stood for impressed us more than his past acquaintanceship with William Carlos Williams.

Mostly we went there to share in what we imagined to be significance and to drink our beer after politely disposing of a thimbleful of Beaudoin's saccharine, decidedly unalcoholic, homemade elderberry wine. That a short, portly, middle-aged man living with his parents read the *I Ching* and wrote haiku in Memphis in the late fifties seems to me remarkable; that he was able to inspire some versifying and self-respect in a multifarious group of young people and never, as far as I know, try to put the make on any of them was exemplary.

After the elderberry wine came the dramatic reading of the poem Beaudoin had written that day — conversational, free-associated, unpolished, eventually to go into a file cabinet with a thousand others. He would throw the coins and read oriental insights that made no sense to me, and launch a discussion of some literary work as encouragement for our artistic endeavors. Then someone would drive him to the cop house. His was a place divorced from family and life in general where you could pretend with impunity. Everybody showed off a bit, Kit included. These displays were either verbal, her mode, or literary, which was mine. Beaudoin gave away little jewels for the best poems written by teenagers in the city; these Gemstone Awards got our names into the newspaper. I received a paste amethyst for a strident bit of Memphis misanthropy, inspired by "Howl," that contained the line "Fill your pockets with shit." Beaudoin changed the offending word to "soot" so I could read the poem in a quavery voice at a ceremony in the Peabody attended by my mother and grandmother.

Beaudoin came to parties in the studio. He got to know my father, who liked him, to my surprise. Beaudoin's good humor and, by Memphis's standards, his outrageousness appealed to Dad. Groups and individuals were unrelated in my father's mind, I realized. He had plenty against Negroes, artists, and homosexuals, until he met one. Then the person replaced the group, the prejudice submerged, and Dad's natural gregariousness took over.

Some of my parents' old friends had moved away, people I remember fondly, the men witty, plump, avuncular, amused by my father's casual but constant jibes, the women accommodating, smiling, touched with a female remove that preserved their pleasantness. Some couples dropped off the social map, possibly because Dad was drinking too much or simply because he didn't cut back with age, as they had. Younger men and women replaced them, my brother's friends whose devotion to my parents sometimes outlasted their close connection to Frank. The studio had played a part in bringing them all to 491 South Highland, but some of my parents' new friendships would outlast that, too.

We are sitting in the living room on a Saturday, and everybody — Mom, Dad, Dodo, Jack, and I — is smoking. Pall Malls, Winstons, Chesterfields, and a Tampa Nugget contribute to a murky stream plowing toward the attic fan, past the coffee table made from a cut-down Victorian sideboard, past Mom's free-form oil of dancers in a void, past the couch set sideways to give the room an appearance of greater breadth. Dodo and Jack are reading. Dad is cleaning his fingernails with his small, bone-handled Case knife. Mom has that dreamy but serious expression associated with large pronouncements.

She says, "I think we've found it, Jimbo."

They have been looking for their own house, off and on, since the Depression.

"I know you don't believe me," she adds. "Tell him, Connie."

"Yes, indeed," says Dad.

"It's a beautiful house, just what I would have designed. That's the amazing thing — it belongs to a landscape architect, a woman. She put in all the latest things. Skylights, hot-air vents, a sculpted patio. We'll have to cut some trees out back, it's just too dark. But everything else is perfect. The furniture's just what I would have picked. Tasteful. We could buy the house without the furniture, but everything fits so well. Some things were made just for it. You're going to love your room. It's airy, with a sliding partition between you and Danny . . ."

"Do I have to move, too?"

I know I shouldn't have said it. I don't even care much, confident that college will take me away, if only to Knoxville, but something extrudes the words like doleful gobs of concrete. Mom looks at Dad, who raises an eyebrow but continues the job at hand. His annoyance with me for failing to show enthusiasm and with Mom for wanting to move extends to real estate agents and banks for charging so much, to the house in which we sit for requiring him to keep it upright for twenty years, to Dodo for marrying Jack, and to President Eisenhower for allowing Richard Nixon to get close to the White House.

"I guess we've made an error," says Mom.

"Oh, honey . . ."

She pushes his words away with splayed fingers. "You try and try, and in the end nobody cares. Nobody gives a damn. I've put my soul into this, and after years of backbreaking searches, when we finally find something suitable . . . Well, you and the boys can just take over. I wash my hands of the whole thing."

She is on her feet, thrusting her cigarette into the heap of butts. I have seen enough of her exits to know that, once launched, they cannot be forestalled. Fixing her gaze on something beyond the wall, beyond the overhanging oaks that she, too, has known since she was a baby, she begins a glide that takes her across the room to the sofa, touched in turning, and with messianic radiance sweeps into the hall.

Dad and I sit in silence, waiting. Out in the kitchen now, Dodo clangs around, putting the vegetable soup on the stove. Her soup is opaque and contains everything left in the refrigerator; I have discovered spaghetti, and peanuts, in Dodo's version. By contrast, my mother's contains precisely cut carrots and celery, lovely canned tomatoes, and browned stew meat as part of a clear assemblage pushing up delectable bits of oil. My mother is one fine cook. Meat — slabs of beef, chicken — and vegetables, including collards, lady peas, and okra, cooked to within an instant of obliteration, are still delicious.

Mom reappears and says, "Personally, I don't give a damn if we end up living *in a tent*."

I knew the Depression had been a bad time because then white men had cut our grass. It was all right to cut your own grass, as Frank and I had been doing for years, but if someone else cut it, and he wasn't black, or a kid, something was seriously amiss. I imagined those unemployed white men in the distant past boarding flatcars in a drab midwestern landscape and riding east, to Normal, and ending up at our screen door, where Dodo handed them bologna on white bread with plenty of mayonnaise. I had no idea what became of unemployed black men during the Depression.

Even by the late fifties the phrase "civil rights" was murky, having more to do with distant courts and the refusal to buy things than with a notion of equality. News of the bus boycott in Montgomery in 1955 had arrived as if from another country. Memphis's Nigras — as they were called by politicians, ministers, and anyone bowing almost imperceptibly to a subtle, nascent awareness — were content, those same people said. Montgomery just couldn't happen there.

Even the troubles in Little Rock in the fall of 1957, just a hundred miles west, barely had impact. Little Rock inspired familiar derogatory remarks about one half of Memphis's population by the other half, but no real apprehension. So segregated was Memphis that relatively few black people lived in white school districts; there was little overlap in shopping or entertainment. The sheen of immutability overlaying everything from prayer breakfasts to Cotton Carnival floats applied equally to race.

No white person growing up in Memphis could have escaped the word "nigger." As a child, if I had heard Purnell refer to one of our maids as a nigger, I would have slugged him. They were somehow part of the family. I never heard my grandmother or my mother use the word, but all males did, at one time or another. It entailed a wide range of emotions. Paternalism was one, viciousness another. Men hanging around gas stations and pool halls often raged against the collective nigger. We all knew about "egging" — driving through Orange Mound and other black neighborhoods at night, lobbing eggs at people on the street — and worse, hurling bottles and even stolen watermelons into the windshields of oncoming jalopies.

To condemn these things was to condemn others in the culture; therefore my friends and I found it irresistible. Like reading books, complaining of racism was a form of rebellion, only more potent and potentially dangerous. Our efforts were pathetic, though. We goaded adults by speaking reverentially of black performers and insisting upon watching them on television, even when we didn't like the music of Ray Charles and Nat "King" Cole; we listened to the acknowledged radio founts of "nigger music," not because we liked it but because it rubbed older people the wrong way.

The continued appearance of *Hambone's Meditations* in the *Commercial Appeal* and other southern newspapers would have been more of an embarrassment to me if I had associated myself with the cartoon. By now I saw the character as a grotesque holdover, a piece of the walking dead no different or more relevant than Yank's phrase "You're wrong about that" and Jack's distinction of having once been the best-dressed man in St. Louis. My mother could not speak now of her father without, at best, a silence in me that was hostile to everything associated with J. P. Alley, with the notable exception of his studio.

Once I walked out of a barbershop to protest the words of an adipose insurance salesman boasting of employing a "boy" to shine his shoes and wash his Studebaker. As a lifeguard I had struck up a friendship with a black waiter named Troy, but the idea that it could have developed into more than idealized conversations about music and girls was preposterous. In Memphis in the late fifties there was nowhere for such a relationship to go, if I had possessed the nerve to push it. There was no common ground.

15

DEBUTANTE PARTIES served a number of needs in Memphis, most of them only tangentially related to matrimony. More than one man had built a house just to contain his daughters' coming-out parties. Debutante affairs formally recognized that girls had grown up, and provided a forum for boys to start thinking about it, all the while affirming the status quo. It was a nice Memphian paradox: acknowledge change while acting to keep things as they are.

The social net was cast wide enough to include the Conaways. Accepting an invitation to a debutante ball wasn't easy. Like fraternities and sororities, they stood in direct opposition to the social and artistic emancipation my friends and I considered ourselves examples of. On the other hand, debutante parties could be fun. They made you feel like an adult. You could drink for free, and being there proved you acceptable on some level to the prevailing order, a satisfaction even if the invitation was rejected.

Usually it wasn't. We railed against the formalities: engraved cards, stilted language, the choice of bands, the occasional request that we accompany a young woman neither beautiful nor racy, the requirement of written acceptance, and the maneuvering of oneself into a tuxedo. Renting these was humiliating, since we didn't really know how they worked and felt the presence of others there before us. But when all was done, when we were properly studded and bow-tied, we felt like Russian princes in the court of the czar.

Sometimes parents went, too. I remember sitting with two girls in crinolines who pretended to be interested in me and looking up to see my mother standing with some other women, watching. I felt debonair, connected, the center of mock attention — a contender. Mom smiled, an indication that she knew what I was feeling and that she felt it, too, that for the moment we shared an illusion and all the possibilities that went with it.

Girls usually made their debuts as college freshmen but spent several seasons practicing. Kit attended most of the parties during our senior year in high school. I went to one at the MCC and stood at the bar at pseudo-ease, hand in pocket, watching the ceremonies out on the ballroom floor. Harley was there in a Navy dress uniform, dark blue with gold buttons and a high collar that set off his large, crew-cut head. We had a drink together, taken from a bottle belonging to the father of the girl who had invited us. Harley told a joke to the assembled stags that in retrospect seems macabre: "People are flying on this jet to Europe, see, and this announcement comes on: 'Ladies and gentlemen, today's flight is entirely electronic. There's no pilot and no copilot. Don't worry, you have nothing to fear . . . to fear . . . to fear . . .'"

He drifted off with the college crowd. Kit had come with one of them, from Sewanee, a Memphis University School graduate who padded the rail with his glen-plaid cummerbund and addressed the bartender by name. Silently I scoffed at his privilege, knowing that after he took Kit home I would enter the Smiths' kitchen door and she and I would take up our passionate meander, toward what we weren't sure, but something the boy from Sewanee wouldn't even get close to. It occurred to me that there might be a female corollary to the male habit of having two girlfriends. Kit was kept busy much of the time by activities and people — including young men — I had only a dim notion of or interest in; our relationship retained a secret character related as much to ideas as to sex, but secret still. I was a public school miscreant and potential dropout, the dreamer in the car port. I didn't see myself that way, but as seer, potentially great commentator in free verse, the one with talent, whereas the competition had only money, connections, decent looks, good grades, and demonstrated athletic ability. And they could dance.

Other girls helped fill the interstices around Kit's absences, but they didn't matter. She was the one I dreamed about, consciously and otherwise; Kit was the only girl I ever saw as a component in that dim conception, life.

That spring I started getting phone calls at home from a boy I didn't know. He'd say, "Conaway?" and I'd say, "Yeah," and he'd say, "I'm gonna beat your ass."

This went on for a couple of months. I hung up each time, until I learned that he was the new boyfriend of my old girlfriend Veronica. Then I made a stab at conversation: "What's wrong?"

"You know what's wrong."

He wanted me to meet him at a White Station burger oasis, where he hung out. I didn't want to do that. Like most boys, I had grown up between fear and the swagger, when at any point you could be challenged, and not just in clubs across the river. The danger of losing your self-respect was equaled by the risk of repulsing a date with a split lip and torn clothes, testaments to a shortfall in this all-American sport. Dad had boxed in school, to learn to handle himself. I still have a pugilist's medal of his, a tiny triangular bit of pewter showing a boxer in an old-fashioned pose and some letters whose meaning is lost. Dad spoke admiringly of men who could fight; I think he exaggerated some of his own. When he came home with his overcoat torn, he said he had knocked a man down who grabbed him by the collar, but I'm not sure this happened. Dad admired Elvis for reportedly punching two hecklers at a gas pump. But his boxing lessons, when I was young, had been mostly verbal: "Keep your hands up, elbows in . . . Move from side to side . . . Don't take your eyes off his eyes." I don't remember ever actually hitting him when wearing the big, puffy gloves kept around just for that purpose.

Two years before, Harley and I had trained briefly for the Golden Gloves, at the fairgrounds, hitting the heavy bag and in elaborate gear going a round or two with someone our own weight, well supervised. I was also swimming the backstroke for Central at the time and caught a cold coming out of the YMCA with wet hair which mercifully removed me from the ring.

Doing battle with a stranger over the favors of a girl I had already had seemed useless. I wasn't at that spot any longer. My life had changed — for the better, I thought. Like fraternities, violence belonged to a dim, paleolithic time, unsuited to my new sensibilities. And now came this reminder of what I had put behind me, this shitass from yesteryear. Didn't he know I was interested in literature?

The people in the Whirlaway that night didn't include members of the older crowd, all off at college. They had taken something vital with them. The same records were on the jukebox, but the lyrics didn't seem pertinent anymore. I felt caught between the familiar and the unknown, without prospects. My friends had been accepted by colleges — Kit by Vassar, Metcalf by the University of North Carolina, Rughead by

Pratt Institute — but not me, not yet, and high school almost over.

"Somebody outside wants to talk to you."

I looked up into the face of a strange boy. He turned and walked out, past the Whirlaway's scarred plywood door. I followed him. Three more strangers waited in the parking lot: Levi's, white T-shirts, that lassitude that precedes violence and makes it worse. I felt a heaviness in my chest. Coordination of hands and feet — walking — was complicated by the beer I had drunk. I wasn't intoxicated but I was befuddled and apprehensive, and I regretted not taking this more seriously, preparing myself.

One boy separated himself from the others. He was shorter than I, but thicker. His mouth hung open, a rictus in the Whirlaway's blue neon glow. He moved around me crabwise and said, "Yeah," dragging the word out. It was the voice from the telephone.

"What do you want?" I asked.

"You know what I want."

We were never going to have a conversation, this guy and I. Standing at an angle to him, my hands down, eyes averted — things you were not supposed to do — I tried to look cool, contained. Some bogus instinct told me to appear to give the problem serious consideration, and it would go away, instead of jumping on it with both feet, as I should have done.

He said something that had the word "Veronica" in it. I gestured, indicating that what was done was done, and then he made a sound like air coming out of a pierced inner tube.

"What?"

". . . fuckinshitI'mgonna . . ."

"Look, punk . . ." I said.

Anyone who has never been badly beaten can't imagine what it's like. There is an order, a regimen of increasing pain only indirectly connected to your own conduct. With your control slipping away comes the realization that the fight may be lost but it is not over, that the other person has only begun to work out what is bothering him and that you are his in a basic, ugly way. Beyond the humiliation lies a black recess in which something of the person you know as yourself hides; you hope some of that person is surviving, but at some point you are no longer sure. Meanwhile the damage, and the noise, goes on.

The first blow landed on the side of my head, that much I remember. I had miscalculated, part fear, part arrogance: I didn't want any kind of relationship with a rogue from White Station. Then we were in the gravel, slinging each other around like sacks of flour. On the ground was not where I wanted to be in a fight. My neck ended up in the crook of his arm, his knuckles defining the planes of my face in furious collisions. I couldn't parry the blows. He sensed my panic and continued to swing, putting his weight into it, pinning my arms tighter. This was not just rogues against frats, not just little cookie-cutter houses in bald developments out beyond Summer Avenue against oak-shaded homes in established neighborhoods and the perception of social superiority; it wasn't just jealousy but a kind of sexual frenzy, and there was no Harley around to drag him off. From an enforced distance I heard the blows, tasted blood; that new sound was my teeth grinding against one another. I felt a finger inside my mouth, trying to tear the flesh.

". . . chicken . . . Say you're chicken . . . Say . . ."

Later, I sat in the gravel. Someone drove me home, I don't know who. In the glare of the upstairs bathroom I saw that my new corduroy jacket had been destroyed; I couldn't look into my own eyes.

Dad appeared, and I turned to confront my nightmare reflected in that familiar, sleepy face. He said, "What in the world, sonny boy . . ." and I said, "I had a fight."

*

The next morning my head looked like someone had stretched a purple stocking over it, with slits for eyes. My lips were rubbery things that bounced off each other when I tried to eat. I spent the day on the couch. Dodo would touch my head in passing; my brother Dan would come in and look at me from time to time, as if at a gruesome museum exhibit. Miraculously, nothing had been broken, but I was damaged in a worse way. I had lost whatever self-respect I had built up since my disastrous eleventh grade. I couldn't stop thinking about how I had lost it, and I couldn't summon up the nerve — the will — to go back to my attacker and set things straight.

I couldn't talk about it, either. Dad allowed that, for a time. He suspected that the viciousness I had been exposed to was related to more than an adolescent squabble. If this had been just another fight, he told me, then somebody should pay. If it had been more than that, he wanted to know what had caused it. Gradually he got around to the subject of Veronica, as I feared he would. Never one to discuss emotions, fastidious in these matters as much out of self-preservation as anything, Dad forced out the question.

"Were you ever, ah, intimate?"

The phrase seemed preposterous to me: Veronica and I had been a lot more than that. I said, "Yes."

There was no reprimand, only the raised eyebrow. Sin was something Dad didn't talk much about. He went to church more for the example than out of conviction; he didn't read the lesson or teach Sunday school at St. John's or do anything outside attending service. He referred to God very occasionally, anthropomorphically, and his prayers before important meals were brief to the point of aphorism. He affirmed conventional morality while expressing extreme views about other things.

Once he had said to me, "Don't make her fall in love with you."

I had interpreted this, and still did, as an indication that Dad was apprehensive about the possible outcome, and maybe jealous. His attitude toward my mother had always struck me as obsessive, more idealistic than physical. I had tried to imagine them in bed, and couldn't, even though I once caught them there on a Saturday afternoon when I was supposed to be at a football game and dropped by the house. They looked sheepish; we all must have looked that way. I sat on the edge of the bed and chatted, the smoother-over of our mutual embarrassment, and went back out to the car feeling peculiar, as if it were I who had been intruded upon.

I suspect that any misbehavior on Dad's part during wartime was alcoholic, not carnal, if indeed there was flesh available in his corner of the South Seas. He did look at women on the street; my brother Dan once asked him about it, and Dad said, "I'm not dead yet." I doubt if there was ever any crossover from the speculative to the real, however. He didn't seem to have it in him. I think the Victorian precepts of his mother and his aunt Mamie were as deeply rooted as Dad's individualism, that although he had been the superannuated frat boy and bon vivant, and in some ways still was, he took his license among other males, not among girls, not that way. Women were lesser beings in need of protection, and marrying, and they could hurt you when they wanted to.

We received a call from the father of the boy who had beaten me up. He came by, a stubby figure in a hat with a narrow brim who sat in the easy chair, gripping the armrests. Dad and I sat on the couch. It was strange, seeing my obscure enemy's father so clearly. He told us his son had been goaded by Veronica's parents into becoming their instrument of retribution for the broken retreat vow, that his son was not very bright and, caught between infatuation with Veronica and jealousy fueled by her parents — I could imagine those Sunday dinners — and afraid of being beaten up himself, had gone a little crazy.

These two fathers, talking their way around things, had something else in common: they agreed, without actually saying so, that I had gotten rather more than enough of what I deserved. I knew that I had been made to pay for Veronica, and accepted at least part of the blame. What the other man really apologized for, in the end, was his son's loss of control, although again, it wasn't put that way. Dad didn't like that part, either. He might have upset all the decorousness of our discussion, but for the sex.

The night of the fight I had dreamed that a great black bird fell from the sky onto the roof of 491 South Highland. When I told Kenneth Beaudoin about the dream, he ascribed it to fear of nuclear attack — bomb shelters were then in vogue — but I knew better. The dream was about death: of the illusions that I was brave, that I could depend on someone other than myself, that anything but getting out of Memphis stood between me and chaos.

16

AFTER HIGH SCHOOL, life in America is one long convalescence. The soft amalgam of imponderables that is home recedes in an acceleration of images that are bright, hard-edged, and, if you're lucky, delivering. That summer mine included Alabama kudzu and, in Florida, as I wrote home, "a long white highway where it takes five rides to travel 200 miles." Pink stucco on the white beach, the weight of aluminum trays piled with dirty dishes, and the smell of ocean blowing through the corner room in the hotel where I waited tables.

Also tough girls from Daytona with stenciled tan lines. Clattering palm fronds. The creased paperback edition of *Lord Jim* and a wad of bills converted to money orders dutifully sent back to help cover college costs. I wrote to Dad on Father's Day apologizing for not sending a present and listing my duties, knowing that a description of work would appeal to him: taking orders and busing dirty dishes three meals a day, mopping the floor, washing and ironing my clothes. "I quit smoking last Monday," I added, "and there isn't anything else to spend my money on . . . My feet have never hurt from working before."

He and I were allied for once against the establishment. When I had applied to the University of North Carolina, Central High had refused to send my transcript to UNC on grounds, I suppose, that I should not be inflicted upon the educational system of a friendly neighboring state. That despite the fact I had "turned things around" — Dad's words — during my senior year. He went to the principal and this time prevailed. Together we had solicited letters of recommendation from Dad's friends, from Beaudoin and anyone else we could think of, and in this brief father-son solidarity moved a mountain.

In late August, Metcalf and I were sitting in a Greyhound bus warming up in the Union Street terminal in Memphis. Our umbrellas were safe overhead — you were nothing in Chapel Hill without a black umbrella — and our new clothes stashed in the hold, mine in Dad's old Navy trunk: crew-neck sweater, cordovans, those paisley ties. Eager for the collegiate fit, we were unwilling to acknowledge that eight hundred miles of reverse transcontinental migration lay between it and us; I will never forget the sight of Metcalf smoking Luckys and gazing out at passing Tennessee as if at a geological conspiracy.

Since I had been accepted late, I was shoehorned into a jock dorm near the gym. In one bunk lay a large Irish presence known as Huey, from Queens, varsity center on the basketball team and a paragon of consideration compared to the varsity guard occupying the bunk under mine. His mother sent him hard sausage from lower Manhattan every month, which he made into sandwiches and then forced underclassmen to buy them. He and Huey made studying a guerrilla activity, until I was able to transfer to another dorm and stop putting out the lights every night at the library.

To Dad, Chapel Hill meant ΠΚΑ and the athletic extravaganzas of one of the great southern party schools. To me, it meant Thomas Wolfe. So sick was I of the "Greek" experience that I skipped rush, something he couldn't understand. Through his contacts Dad arranged for me to be privately appraised anyway, and I sat for an hour in the ΠΚΑ house in Chapel Hill with a button-down replica of a hundred Memphians. Not only did the mock heroics seem shopworn and stupid; they suggested that loud, false fealty, beer chugging, and date repulsing were inescapable accoutrements of life beyond Memphis.

Mom wrote urging me to pledge, and blamed my apparent misanthropy on "outside reading." In a single letter she advocated having a good time ("Fun and kicks are a very *important* part of living") but warned against drinking; told me not to worry about the expense of a fraternity but to spend my money "wisely" (i.e., on something other than fun and kicks, which was what fraternities were all about); to study hard but not "too hard"; to be careful in my choice of friends but not too "narrow and closed-in." Every bit of advice had its antidote, a reflection of her own attempts to avoid "a sick outlook on life." I admit that some of the more exhausting letters went into the wastebasket unread.

My sole objective was staying in school. I possessed — I don't know why — an incandescent but unarticulated faith that things would turn out all right if I could just get launched. There was comfort in heavy volumes of European history, English composition (the subject of our essays was, of all things, the battle of Shiloh), even my rudimentary French text. Carrying them across campus on football weekends, I would encounter whole families there for the tribal intensity of a Carolina home game. Fathers would stop and stare at me, as if carrying books on a Saturday was worse than bad luck — it was bad manners.

Beyond the quad, beyond the traditional oaks and red brick Georgian propriety, was the beer-sloshed bar and deli,

Harry's, used by a relatively small but active group of artists, writers, and academics closeted in scarred booths. UNC set a precedent for southern campuses at the end of the fifties, a liberal enclave in a state as segregated and as bound to the past as any. It included respected departments of English and journalism; it drew "known writers" — Paul Green, Betty Smith — as well as assorted misfits.

Harry's on-campus adjunct was the *Carolina Quarterly*, run by the ebullient red-headed Nancy, who had brought with her from New York the ideal blend of softness and big-city candor. Literary dame, pavement mother, she took in Metcalf and me as deep southern comers — Memphis was, after all, the de facto capital of Mississippi — and escorted us to a party on the alley above the Rathskeller that transcended haiku and elderberry wine: prodigious amounts of dago red from jugs, Israeli folk songs, young women in leotards and no makeup sucking smoke out of their cigarettes, bearded men the sight of whom stopped traffic on University Avenue, all on the landing outside the narrow, book-cluttered apartment of an aspiring novelist named Ralph Dennis.

Just out of the Navy and a beneficiary of the GI Bill, Ralph had a pocked, friendly south Georgia face and a large capacity for the profane and for helping other, younger writers. Ralph had been to Korea; he was worldly and entitled the way people were who had experience — any experience. He said that fiction was the only kind of writing equal to contemporary life, and that I should pursue it to the exclusion of poetry and most everything else; I took this wisdom with me back to the dorm, where I threw up, this time over the edge of my bunk. Carolina's high-scoring guard managed to roll out of the way. He forgave me the near miss, but never my ignorance of conference basketball.

I got a part-time job in the student union handing out Ping-Pong paddles and piping classical music into a room backlit by soft Carolina evenings. Deep carpets and deeper sofas, card tables, and dour grad students slapping chess clocks. The rest of the time I studied. My interim grades showed me passing in "stars for jocks" (astronomy), social science, hygiene, and math, with an "excellent" in French. When I told Dad about this, he said, "You're not having a good enough time." The absence of a fraternity still rankled.

I lean against the pea-green dorm wall, telephone grafted to my ear, listening to Kit's voice rather than her words. I have that peculiar brand of homesickness that fastens on people rather than place, a movable feast of misery. The distance between us seems intergalactic. We make plans to meet in New York at Thanksgiving.

Metcalf, four other boys, and I got into an old sedan and headed north on state roads, stopped for supper at someone's house in Washington, D.C., and reached the city at midnight. Somehow Metcalf and I wedged ourselves into Rughead's room at Pratt. New York was the ultimate human experience, I knew, but all I could think of was Kit, to be met under the clock at the Biltmore Hotel, in traditional fashion. The next day I found the hotel lobby, crowded with college students who knew each other and obviously had big plans. Kit materialized in knee socks, dark sweater, scarf, and trench coat. Beautiful gunmetal hair. We embraced, and someone said of Kit, "Who the hell's that?"

"What should we do?" I asked.

"Let's walk."

Over to Park Avenue, uptown, across, downtown. We talked about school, summer plans, and study abroad. Kit seemed older, unfazed by the sight of the Chrysler Building, by all of New York. She had been here before, no doubt with more direction and entertainment than I could provide. There was the question of money, as always. We counted ours, and walked on until a restaurant appeared that looked friendly: banquettes, people sitting side by side, smiling headwaiter. Then the awful menu. We ordered fancy hamburger steak, which came with green peas and what I remember as mashed potatoes made to look like flowers. We each had a glass of pink wine.

I said, "I had a poem accepted. By the *Carolina Quarterly.*"

This was a triumph: focused intimacy, clear lines to genius and future triumphs. Unfortunately we couldn't talk about it in the abstract forever. Kit said, "I want to read it."

I had brought a copy but knew better than to let her read it now: criticism tended to follow readings.

She said, "A funny thing happened to me at a house party. I went to bed and this boy who was supposed to be my date came into my room. He was naked."

I imagined an estate with stone walls, more girls in knee socks, boys in letter sweaters. Old-fashioneds; a discussion of the Kingston Trio. I was jealous but also envied his directness and what was apparently endless opportunity, and realized that there was a degree of confidence I would never possess and a realm of experience I would never know.

All I said was "Ah."

"I told him to get out. He acted like it was a joke. Then he called me Little Miss Grits." *That* got Kit's attention.

After dinner we walked some more. She was returning to Vassar the next day. Papers, upcoming exams, incredible pressures. Kit intended to show these northerners that Little Miss Grits had the brains. We got back to the Biltmore before midnight. "What about . . ." I said.

"I've got roommates, Jim. Besides," she said, and kissed me, "I'll see you in Memphis."

The day I arrived home for Christmas, Dad came into my room before dinner and asked, "Bourbon or scotch?"

My brother had been asked the same question on his first

day home from college — at breakfast. So had Dad, his first time back in Memphis from Washington and Lee. A returning freshman was almost a man, entitled to a drink with his parents; it didn't matter that he had been drinking for years.

In February, I moved out of the dorm at UNC and into a one-room apartment many blocks from campus, beyond the farthest-flung frat house. I shared it with a philosophy grad student named Bailey, part of the loose affiliation hanging out at Harry's. The apartment belonged to a traveling salesman transferred back to Atlanta, and reflected a peculiar version of sentimental southernness: phony crossed sabers on the wall, phony antique mirrors with gilt frames, gold drapes, phony French provincial furniture, and some oils of the ancestor school. "I know Dad's sweating by this time and looking down the letter for the rent," I wrote my parents, "which is the clincher. It only costs $18.50 a month" — three dollars less than the dorm.

In fact, the apartment was in a leaky frame house with walls so thin the gold drapes swayed when the wind blew. There was one bathroom for four other tenants, including a paraplegic and a very bad painter named Ross, who had no refrigerator and kept food in covered pots until it putrefied. Bailey, a hulking Kentuckian, harbored some powerful contradictions: he played classical piano, and in bad moments picked fights with football players. He talked reverentially about fresh air in the Appalachians, and chain-smoked Camels. Every morning after his alarm clock went off I would hear his large, spatulate feet hit the boards, followed by the scrape of a wooden match and a release of the essence of Turkish tobacco. Then a quote from Nietzsche or, occasionally, Kierkegaard. He would haul on work pants bought in a farm supply store and a sweater and set off for campus, still smoking, books clutched behind him, head thrust forward like a contemporary backcountry Beethoven.

The oil ran out in March and we lived without heat until the weather turned. I piled every extra piece of clothing I owned, including the ties, onto my bed. When Dad heard of this he objected on grounds that the human mind won't function when cold. We held parties attended by many of the same people I had met at Ralph's. The few girls who came my way were either older — tough, ersatz beatniks — or grad students more enamored of Chaucer or Jacobean drama than of impoverished underclassmen. Women were a precious commodity in general, disallowed entirely as freshmen and sophomores at UNC and admitted only in limited numbers as juniors and seniors. Pigs' paradise, Bailey called it.

On those nights we dined in together, Bailey would set an unopened can of soup or beans in a pot of boiling water and extract it at the precise moment before it exploded. Heating it this way meant we didn't have to wash the pan. We envied our neighbor Ross his six-foot auburn-haired girlfriend, who visited him once a week. They made love on Ross's mattress and springs shoved up against the common wall; Bailey and I would sit in our freezing, cut-rate replica of the nineteenth-century Georgian genteel and watch the wall shake. The tiny crack I noticed in the mirror hanging there when I moved in would lengthen to five feet by the time I moved out.

Kit came to visit in April, the highlight of spring semester. I booked her into the Carolina Inn and met her at the airport, having arranged to borrow a car. I remember my nervousness most clearly. I refused to hand Kit's handsome blackwatch-plaid suitcase to the bellhop so I wouldn't have to tip him. I could see disapproval on the face of the desk clerk as Kit and I ascended the stairs.

Within a minute we were on the bed, alone at last in a hotel room. I held her, aware of just how lonely I had been, eager to try again. Then the telephone rang and the desk clerk said, "You'll have to do your visiting in the lobby."

We went to Harry's — small-time, I supposed, compared to Kit's life up north. I needn't have worried. She had made the dean's list and thrived on the artistic disagreements that fueled Harry's commerce in hot pastrami and three-point beer, arguing authoritatively about existentialism and Cuba, enhancing my own standing by association. She even took issue with Ralph's assertion that female Victorian novelists were a waste of time.

We ate pizza with a poet named Parker and went to a party together. Parker later wrote a poem about Kit that contained the line "There was money in her voice." I didn't know that it was first F. Scott Fitzgerald's line. I was both pleased that Parker was impressed with Kit and incensed by the suggestion that money had anything to do with it.

Bailey had agreed to spend the night out. Kit was amused by the sabers on our wall, but I had the impression that she found my apartment depressing and my life in Chapel Hill too narrow — my mother's warning. We played music and lay together for hours, touched by the ghost of Memphis. Because we hadn't made love there, it suddenly seemed unlikely that we would anywhere.

I worked in the Colorado Rockies that summer, having graduated from waiter to desk clerk, in a former mining town where the lode was now tourism. Among the attractions were a painting of The Face upon the Barroom Floor, the Metropolitan Opera's summer version of *Aida*, and dime beers in the Gulch. I didn't last the season, for I had determined to go on to California. "I guess I have some great hunk of immaturity that I'm never going to get rid of," I wrote to my parents, touched with westering melodrama, "for it has become obvious to me by now, and probably to you, that I can't stay in one place for very long at a time . . . I guess everybody looks for something, some harder than others, and it doesn't seem I have found any semblance of mine, whatever it may be. You are about as understanding as parents could be, and that is the greatest thing I have . . . I could feel the disappointment in Pop's voice, but I knew before I called that he wouldn't object."

I think my being in the West reminded Dad of his experiences there and touched some expansive part of him rarely revealed in a systematic way. Out of character, on the old Underwood, he wrote a letter from Memphis, a kind of homegrown stream of consciousness that I read in Central City and kept with me on the trip to California and then back on the Greyhound from Los Angeles to Memphis. He would never again write anything like it:

"As your Dad, I'd like to tell you some things Life has taught me, and what I consider important. First of all, my family is my life. Smoking is habit-forming — drinking can be relaxing and fun if properly handled and indulged in only on occasion, but can become an insidious habit . . . Sex is wonderful — work is rewarding — education is a necessary pleasure — money is a must — culture is desirable — a sound body and mind is both a delight and a needed thing — leisure is a luxury and youth is the time to get all these things turned straight and not set up a damned fool's life based on any one or any group of them. Christ was a wonderful man — God *is* there and is the boss. Our country is the most ideal place on this ole earth to live (although it can use some patching from time to time).

"Love and understanding of the other person and the giving to him [of] something that he didn't have when he came across you fulfill the desires, pleasures and ambitions of a man."

September, back in Chapel Hill, I rented a room in a widow's house near campus. I found life less interesting than the year before, and lonely. There still weren't enough girls, and some of my friends had left, including Metcalf, who had transferred to Southwestern, in Memphis. My brother had graduated from Southwestern, and that school seemed a good enough, and easy, choice for me. While there I could live at home and save everybody money. I could finish off my undergraduate career amidst the familiar, which was always more appealing from a distance, something I seemed unable to remember until I got home again. It was disastrous reasoning, and deep down I knew this, but I decided to transfer in the spring.

I returned to New York at Thanksgiving but this time didn't tell anyone, including Kit. I stayed with a woman I had met in Central City, a member of the Met's ballet corps, cocooned in her apartment on West 96th Street.

Kit made her debut that Christmas at the MCC. First she and the other girls received instruction from a woman who had been training debutantes for years: what to wear, and when, the protocol of presentation — debutantes chose two escorts — and how to make the proper exit. Individual and general guest lists were scrutinized and any name even vaguely Jewish eliminated. Kit later told me that a name came up, something like Bertrand Hamilton Jones IV, that no one would claim. The advisor decided to invite Bertrand Hamilton Jones IV anyway, because "I like the sound of his name."

Kit's eyes narrowed to black creases when she talked about this. She wanted to drop out, but that would have embarrassed her parents and set an alarming precedent. "It's so *stupid,*" she said, a word that covered a lot of ground with Kit.

I was to be one of her escorts. The other was Sandy Covington, a regular at the Smiths', a garter wearer and perennial accompanier of acceptable young women. He and I were to pick up Kit on the big night, safely deliver her to the club, and appear as flankers for Kit's walk down the center of the ballroom floor and into official matrimonial eligibility. We were to dance with her and with her mother, if Mrs. Smith wanted to dance.

Whatever was left of my connection to social Memphis dissolved that night. So did the special link between Kit and me, if a moment can be found for that. Our relationship had been about innocence more than anything else, about an expanding view of the world and our place in it, without the blinders and defeats of home. It hadn't proved equal to life away from, or back in, Memphis. We would go on seeing each other sporadically, inconclusively, for years but we were already headed for different places, bound up in diverging dreams.

Triumphal music played as individual debutantes swept the length of the ballroom, guarded by their young men in black. When Kit's turn came, I stayed in the bar. It was a spontaneous lapse, if lapses can be spontaneous, and inexcusable. Afterward, Kit came and stood across the room and looked at me. She smiled — sad, amused, ironic. I see her like that now, though the dress, the furniture, and the other people are long gone.

Her mother said, when she finally found me, "Well, Jim, you certainly were conspicuous by your absence." But that was all she said. After all, I had been drinking. It wasn't my fault.

17

IMAGINARY LINES partition all hometowns. These inner frontiers survive age and experience and the physical destruction of their own landmarks. For me, the eastern limits of knowable Memphis will always be the intersection of Poplar and Central avenues, beyond which lies a strangeness that was new when I viewed it as a kid from the saddle of my stripped Schwinn: subdivisions and the ancestors of contemporary malls, an office building or two poking out of the vernal homogeneity that is Memphis, as essential as sticky asphalt and water-laden air in summer, the smell of moldering leaves in winter, and always an afternoon light that hardens and flattens reality.

It was out there that my parents had found their rancher, set back from the street amidst much greenery. The neighbors seemed to have an aversion to photosynthesis, since they were rarely seen outdoors. The first time I went there I felt the chill of the brick floor through my loafers. The living room chairs, made out of wire with deep canvas bellies, were comfortable once you got into them; the wall of open shelves had a clean, modern look enhanced by skylights. The three bedrooms contained by the house were really two, one for my parents and the other, ostensibly, for Dan and me, separated by the sliding partition. Since Frank was teaching in Ohio, and soon to be married, this would suffice. The windows cranked out onto another shady lawn, the only similarity between the Conaways' new, monolevel residence and the house at 491 South Highland.

In the last few years before my parents moved, the old house had begun to slip. Dodo had refinanced and had begun to forgo the upkeep, to save money to meet the bank's note. She had written from St. Petersburg to my father, a year or so before my parents moved, with some sad, specific economies that included letting the fence go "except the trellis that holds up the grapevine and rose bushes . . . Don't think I don't appreciate all the care you and Kathryn give the old place; but if we have to sell it we lose all that."

Dad had been paying sixty dollars a month rent for years; now he was his own domestic boss. And he had a mortgage, a new experience for him, one he didn't care for. The only real financial advice he ever gave me, and that potentially disastrous, was to tell me years later not to buy a house. "You'll never get out from under those payments," he said. But he loved the prospective projects inherent in this acquisition.

My mother felt stylish there, free of the reminders of the past, of the stigma — in her sister's and probably her brothers' eyes — of living in their father's house, and of Jack. She and Dad could have furnished the new house, at least in part, with overflow from the old, but so eager was Mom for genesis that they bought all the furniture, too. She had plans for an addition, part guest bedroom and part studio, with northern light for her easel and a place for Dad's tools and bench. Without the addition it was still a pleasing, eminently livable place, where impromptu parties spilled naturally onto the patio and we all saw ourselves well reflected in the long glass wall.

I moved out not long after I had moved in, blaming the sound of the television set that carried too easily through tasteful paneling, but that was only part of the problem. Obsessed with home when away from it, I wanted to be elsewhere when there. I must have seemed chronically unappreciative and unfocused to my parents. Differences with them over career, friends, and attitude that could be skated over in correspondence tripped us all up when I was home. And it seemed to me that Dad was drinking a bit too much. Mom talked about painting, bought more brushes, oils and canvas, and lamps designed to throw the proper light, took courses at the Memphis Art Academy and subscribed to another art correspondence course, and then didn't paint. This caused tension even when not commented upon. Her physical complaints, some justified, some certainly imaginary, seemed to increase along with those related to housework she still considered excessive even though Dolly had made the eastward transition with her. Mom became something of a specialist in that burgeoning class of drugs designed and prescribed to ameliorate the ordinary. Only Dan went about his business of being a twelve-year-old with enthusiasm and no regrets.

I sought refuge at Dodo's. Back in my old room on Highland, I missed the feeling of many people in a limited space. Dodo and Jack were older, their quirks — Jack's for walking "to town," Dodo's for scrambling the pages of the newspaper when she read it — familiar but pathetic. Much of the past was missing from the house: the Rudisill/Conaway Victorian crystal, Mom's paintings, Frank's books, Dan's bicycle. The neighborhood's commerce hung over our hedge now, serving Memphis State's apparently boundless success. There was real traffic; it no longer felt like Normal, Tennessee.

Every day I traveled across town to class in Dodo's old Plymouth, or hitchhiked, as I had done when at Central. Southwestern excelled at preparing high school graduates from the Delta and elsewhere in the South for life there. Gothic stone buildings put up at great expense maintained the proper English academic remove, or appeared to, but for all their traditional beauty seemed irrelevant. Administrators and many of the teachers — those good, gray Presbyterians — saw to it that we attended chapel and were introduced to the classics. It was a perfectly acceptable place but it was not for me. I had been away; I had seen the elephant, and I felt stuck in a backwater, in a swarm of uneasy associations.

Early one morning I heard a car creep into the driveway. I got up and went to the window to see Harley Laird relieving himself in my back yard. Next to him stood a black four-door Cadillac, the replacement for the silver Pontiac.

I got dressed and went downstairs. "Hey, Con," he said when I came outside. I hadn't seen him in almost two years.

Sprawled in the back seat of the Cadillac was Tad Mullins, one of Harley's more enduring companions, an impoverished ladies' man who during high school had developed good connections. Droll, unperturbable, Tad was drifting among local colleges, a semester here, another there, looking for a good harbor and avoiding the shores of employment. The dark-haired girl next to him shared Tad's bleary-eyed determination that the party wasn't over. "Hey, man," he said, "I want to show her your studio."

I shouldn't have agreed to it but I did. Dodo and Jack were asleep; it was a good hour until daylight. Harley and I watched Tad and the girl teeter past the trellis, and then we got into the Cadillac and sped south on Highland, Harley talking as if our last conversation had just been interrupted. He had a year to go at Annapolis, he said, and then on to flight school; he was going to be a fighter pilot and shoot down MiGs in foreign skies, probably somewhere over Indochina.

I saw a car approaching the intersection at Park Avenue. "Harley," I said, "the light's red."

"Watch this son of a bitch try to bluff me."

We plowed through and the other car rocked to a halt, the driver having the good sense not to blow his horn. Harley's tie was undone and his shirt unbuttoned, revealing a lot of chest. His eyes were bloodshot. He said, "They're asking for it," or similar words.

"Who?"

"The Communists."

We thought about that. Then he said, "They're just using 'em."

"Using who?"

"The Chinks."

We stopped at a diner. I was still not fully awake and drank coffee while Harley forked in eggs, bacon, grits, and biscuits. The Communists were challenging us all over the world, he explained, but particularly in a place called Vietnam. I didn't really know what he was talking about. President Kennedy had been inaugurated in January; he and the First Lady had about them a lightness associated with the new menthol cigarette ads. After the election, caught up in reports of Kennedy's youth and enthusiasm, I had dreamily imagined myself working in some way to help fulfill his dream without knowing what that dream was or what Kennedy represented, except that many older Memphians didn't like him.

"We're gonna kick ass over there," Harley said. "You wait and see. If we don't, the whole goddamn place'll go."

I felt isolated, deprived, stupid. Harley was part of some great enterprise, just touching down in Memphis on the way to glory. I didn't want to share that journey but I did envy him his connection to elsewhere.

We rode back in silence, the night beginning to catch up with him, and found Tad and the girl fumbling with their clothes in a thin dawn raucous with birdsong. Staring at a naked girl was not a common practice even in Harley's crowd, but this one didn't seem to mind. "Why don't you ever come around?" Tad asked me. "Have a drink. Get laid." He laughed apologetically and added, "No offense," as he handed the girl her blouse.

Tad would go on to marry a Miss Hutchinson's graduate who belonged to a wealthy family and then to make book out of her father's office. One weekend Tad would try to corner the football pool, playing banker and refusing to pass along the bets, a weekend when Memphis State beat Ole Miss and UT beat Alabama and all the hometown money was riding on those long shots. Tad would have to flee to the Caribbean owing a million dollars, and his good friends, including some of those he owed, would mourn the fact that they wouldn't be partying anymore with Tad.

I never saw either one of them again. I heard that Harley had a run-in at Annapolis involving marijuana, and survived it. Then that he married a southern blonde and had a child, and was preparing to assume his father's standing at the MCC when he got out of the Navy. Then, at the controls of a sophisticated plane, after Vietnam had become a too familiar place name, that on a bombing mission he went nose-first into a blue lagoon just short of the jungle, and that his body wasn't recovered. I can't claim to have mourned for Harley. I half expected such an end, and felt sorry for him in a more immediate way, saw in my mind's eye his big hunched shoulders and heard his amplified voice: "Oh, shhhiiiiiiiiiit!" I couldn't completely believe in Harley's death until, many years later, I ran my finger over the precise angles of his name, cut into the black marble of the Vietnam Memorial.

That summer I got an introduction to the newspaper business. Linoleum etched with the charred silhouettes of cigarette butts, clamorous telephones, wire baskets full of paper that had to be moved to other wire baskets. I was one of those who did the moving, and brought up cardboard containers of coffee and cigarettes from the restaurant on the ground floor and set them in front of men in shirtsleeves who chewed cigars and made comments cynical by Memphis standards. I regularly descended to the pressroom for copies of each edition, pushed out in waves along rollers and scooped into piles by tough white kids from north Memphis. Sometimes I ascended to the composing room with last-minute copy changes, to see proof-readers jammed together, and stooped typesetters sitting at machines that wheezed and clanked and extruded bits of metal that ended up in inky steel monuments to each printed page. The smell of hot lead vitally linked all that activity and the cerebral intercourse and paper shuffling below to industrial reality: the sight of delivery trucks pulling away from the loading docks on the ground floor and into the glow of the lamps along Union Avenue.

The *Commercial Appeal* had moved its headquarters away from Second and Court streets since my grandfather's hey-day. But in the dark paneling and opaque glass of the private offices I felt a kind of presence. The big corner office contained my uncle Frank, the editor, who would emerge on occasion to honk an order at the city desk; then you could hear the pencils drop. I was still scared of him, of his worldliness and his detailed questions that seemed miraculously pertinent. There were strict standards in the presentation of news, just as there were in bourbon.

My uncles, and the powdery women who put out the Soci-ety section, clearly belonged to a different order there. So did I, I suppose, but this didn't affect the way I was treated, or my view of the place. I considered the newspaper hopelessly reac-tionary. For all our much-discussed roots in the fourth estate, my family seemed to have little in common with those who actually shaped the product, men like the city editor — pro-fane, emaciated, known for caressing with his tongue the filters of the sixty-odd cigarettes he smoked every day, and for collecting Elvis records. The managing editor, a short, strutting man with a black toothbrush mustache and an expression of immutable petulance, never spoke in anything less than a shout. This was a man's world, with a hierarchy and a behavior — demonstrably tough — as prescribed as any court's.

Facts were the currency. The star reporter, Tom, had pale, fishy eyes shaded by the brim of his hat, a permanent appendage. His detachment and his monosyllabic responses to the most dreadful civic developments were legendary, like his drinking in the Press Club across Union Avenue. I saw Tom in action when a handful of black children threatened to enter a white school in midtown and white people thronged in sullen anticipation. I was sent there the way copy boys sometimes were, in case some factual nugget slopped over the edge of the official reporters' collective perception. Stunned by the possibility of actually writing something in a notepad, I hung around the crowd trying to figure out whom I should talk to, and how. The Negroes, under the direction of a disconcertingly calm, nondescript black man in a raincoat, stood in a group surrounded by police; approaching them was unthinkable. Then a cab rolled up and Tom got out, and he and the man in the raincoat walked down an alley to talk, and Tom took some notes. So that's how it's done, I thought.

The story, if reported, was buried in the newspaper. Integration sidled in through the back door because the powers in the city agreed beforehand to keep it out of the forefront of news, another bit of Memphis paternalism. A handful of black people tried to attend a Sunday service at Second Presbyterian, assisted by some white students from Southwestern, and church members sought to get those students expelled. My friend Metcalf joined a group attempting to integrate the lunch counter at Woolworth's, but it, too, failed after the waitress fainted.

Memphis State agreed to admit a few black students. The dean told the assembled white ones, "These Negroes say they want an education. We're going to offer them the opportunity to get the education they *say* they want. You aren't to interfere in any way with their pursuing the education they *say* they want . . . There's going to be no trouble here. If any of them so much as says 'Good morning' to you, I don't want you saying anything back."

When James Meredith enrolled at Ole Miss, we heard the transport planes carrying troops to be convoyed to Oxford come in low over Memphis. The next day Southwestern's brittle dean told the assembled students, "There's no reason to go down there," as if integration in Mississippi were a carnival, not history.

The young men who had passed through college in the fifties, ahead of me, had more in common with my father. Technically I belonged to the same generation but in fact was separated by a divide that would widen with the pressure of drugs, the Beatles, no-regrets sex, and Vietnam. I and my friends still in college, on the edge of the sixties, had a foot on both sides, pulled at by old post–World War Two verities and by the opportunities and dangers inherent in the next social order. But the perspective that made us contemptuous of the contradictions in our fathers' world would also make us suspicious of the revolutionary certitudes and pieties of the new age. We were in a sense the nowhere generation.

One night I went to my parents' for dinner and was met inside the doorway by Dad, who said, "Here's a letter for you."

It was from a friend in Chapel Hill I had written to, about my life in Memphis. "Who opened it?" I asked.

"I did."

"Why?"

Dad said, "What's this peyote business?"

I had read Aldous Huxley's *The Doors of Perception,* a fundament for what became the drug culture. After reading it, a friend and I bought some cacti by mail order from Texas, boiled them on the stove, squeezed them in one of his girlfriend's stockings, and drank a pint of revolting green bile mixed with grapefruit soda. I lay in Overton Park for an hour, waiting for something to happen. Later, while eating ham and eggs in a diner on Monroe Avenue, I noticed tiny mouths in the meat blowing grease bubbles and felt the diner shuttling merrily along nonexistent rails, and knew something was up. But when the landscape turned sinister, where I most wanted to be was home.

"So you read it," I said.

"I asked you a question."

"It was an experiment. Why did you read my letter?"

"I don't want you using drugs."

"I don't use drugs. *Why did you read it?"*

My reaction surprised him and let some air out of his indignation. We never discussed the peyote or the opened letter, just as we never discussed anything important that held the promise of conflict, as most things did by now, from integration to the draft. I tried to make excuses for Dad — that he was worried about me, for instance — but they didn't hold up. I knew he had opened the letter not because he thought I was in psychological trouble but because he was curious. And in his eyes, he had the right.

In that small, bitter violation lay strands of the culture: this was the last, lingering moment of the Adult in America, the monarch whose omnipotence comes by virtue of age and masculinity and not much else, a false entitlement shared by Dad's entire generation that would be swept away in an angry social tide I can't claim to have foreseen or to have taken a significant role in. He and other white men had grown up doing pretty much as they pleased, always addressed as "sir," knowing no one else had a real say in the way things were done. None other than white men deserved explanations for the things white men did, and I wasn't one yet.

Dodo talked about putting her house on the market. Our strip of Highland Avenue had finally been zoned commercial, a financial windfall, and a disaster. People talked about making a killing, a pathetic concept that in reality meant paying off the bank and buying a smaller house in a nondescript neighborhood farther east and having enough left over for a kind of life. "It's too good an opportunity to pass up," Dodo was told by her children and by my father. She would be free of the note, free of the upkeep of a house too big for the two of them, free, they suggested, of all worries.

Selling made good sense, and it made no sense at all. Social Security plus Dodo's savings could have seen them through in the house designed by her father, where her husband had made his reputation, where she had raised her children and helped raise some of her grandchildren, where in close to half a century the red oaks in the yard had become a landmark.

As in most such cases, the decision was really about the American illusion of renewal, of cutting loose. Even Dodo fell for it. With the extra money there would be trips again, not just to St. Petersburg but also to Bucks County, in greater style; there would be a new neighborhood with new friends, a new car, maybe even a membership in one of the minor country clubs like Chickasaw. And it came about the way those things always do: an offer that, because it's more than the owner expects, is accepted, followed by the realization that the property was sold too cheaply, and by the shaking heads of those who pushed so hard to sell in the first place, and by comments like, "Who would have thought they could get *that much* by reselling so quickly?" and, in the end, "Too bad you didn't wait."

Dodo and Jack found a bungalow out east, two small bedrooms and a small living room with a dining "nook" off a tiny kitchen. There was a little screened porch they would never use, and a bare, fenced back yard that ran to the edge of a drainage ditch. Dodo and Jack were now on the wrong side of the tracks, but no one in the family mentioned this. Instead they pointed out that the house was the perfect size and close to my parents, and the neighbors friendly even though a few owned boats up on trailers.

The day they moved out of 491 South Highland, a kind of tribal unburdening occurred, a southern potlatch involving my uncles and aunts and every cousin in Memphis. Cars arrived singly and in pairs; most of us helped load the moving van, and then the dissemination began. I remember my cousins carrying armloads of stuff out of the house and fitting it into their trunks, articles of collective family ownership that Dodo and Jack could not accommodate in their new home, things that should have been judiciously parceled out but weren't because Dodo was understandably distracted and no other adult had the stomach for the job. Here the lack of authority, the absence of a successor to J. P. Alley, finally became clear thirty years after his death. Objects that I had grown up with, as much a part of my inner landscape as my own face in the bathroom mirror but which the Conaways had no clear title to, went out the door and into oblivion. Some that we had claim to as well.

Almost everyone, myself included, got into the spirit. We were shucking a past we didn't understand or need: familiar things, rooms empty for the first time, with odd, exposed angles, views of leaves and lawn and some bit of roofline, the smell of ancient pipe smoke in the studio, the feel of the brass strap handle on the heavy green door, the sigh the door made when I snugged it shut for the last time.

When the furniture was gone from the big house and the place gave back the breath of rejection that abandoned homes do, Dodo and I found ourselves alone in the living room. I suppose Jack was waiting in their new bungalow; my father and other assorted relatives were following the moving van toward it. Dodo's sack dress and usual air of efficiency covered a so far unsuspected sorrow. She turned to survey the bare floors and without warning slumped against the door and began to cry. It was a characteristic sort of grief — unspoken, economic, uncompromising. I felt like crying as well. I put my arms around a surprisingly soft old woman who had traveled west in a wagon and had shot a cigar out of her father's mouth, whose stories about those things had provided twenty years of vital background noise. I said words I hoped were brave and not completely irrelevant, my own wretchedness complicated by the suspicion that something important was ending and the knowledge that a person more authoritative — more capable — than I should be there to offer her comfort. The unceremoniousness of the move left us both displaced and suddenly aware that the condition was terminal.

Among the objects that disappeared into the maw of the move — departed from this life — were a set of moose antlers, my grandfather's pens and pipe rack, odd fossils and geological specimens. Worst loss of all were those flawed green glass fishing floats my father so proudly brought back from the Pacific.

18

IT WAS EXACTLY two decades after the house was sold that my father's mental turbulence became obvious. My trip down from Washington that November, the harrowing drive home in the rain, the distress in my mother's voice, all merged in a discordant sadness that affected subsequent visits and must be familiar to many families. Our denial of any basic, irremedial malady became eventual acquiescence in its existence, and included the odd grief you feel for someone who is both gone and still with you. This was followed by anger at the apparent randomness of the thing and at its medical handlers, and then by a reluctant, calcified sorrow resembling the one we had all originally felt.

Depriving Dad of his car was a watershed and, for him, a catastrophe. He had in his later years favored fast coupes, not for drag racing or even speeding, both of which he abhorred, but solely for their potential. He had earlier owned a little floor-shift Camaro famous for its torque, capable of slithering all over the road if you put the hammer down, sold finally to one of the mechanics who regularly walked out to the gas pumps and opportuned him. The removal of his present car had to be discussed repeatedly with my mother, who had become Dad's sole advocate in the matter, orchestrated and then brought off like a felony. My brother Dan drove it away on the pretext that it had to be worked on, sold it without telling Dad, and gave the money to my mother.

Occasionally Dad would glimpse the car in the roiled waters of his memory, the symbol of freedom and mental as well as physical mobility, and demand, "Where are my car keys?"

Then, "Where the hell is my *car?*"

My mother would say, "Dan has it," or "It's being repaired," and, eventually, "It's not here, Connie."

His response, a summation of a lifetime's worth of annoyance, a railing against cosmic incompetence, and at last a tacit recognition of just how much he had lost, remained thoroughly in character: "Oh . . . nuts!"

Back in Washington, waiting for a formal diagnosis of Dad's predicament, I telephoned Memphis almost every day. Setting aside my work at the *Post,* I would reconnect with a past that seemed, in contrast to the remorseless present circumscribing my writing and my life then, incredibly distant. My mother would say, "Hi, baby," or "Hello, Jimbo," a less enthusiastic response. She was dependent upon my father's mood and would pass along the receiver, and Dad and I begin a conversation notable for its free associations. I would say something like, "How're you feeling?" and Dad would say, "Oh, fine," and there would be a pause. Subsequent questions shot us into the unknown, where a discussion of the weather was really one about birds, or the supermarket, without antecedents or direction; a sentence started by Dad about the lawn mower became an impressionistic rendering of something he saw out the window, or on the shelf next to the telephone, at first subtly, then doggedly, irrelevant.

The fact that he forgot what he had said seconds before embarrassed him, but, being Dad, he never discussed or even alluded to the problem. It got worse. I could feel his pain carried on thousand-mile electronic impulses, the result of a failure of related circuits, these in the soft indecipherables of his brain, as tender and unreliable as the surrounding technology was efficient. I would try to keep up with him, leaping from subject to subject in a surreal matching of words with the imponderables of human association, taking up any one of an infinite number of suggestions that arrived at the confabulatory edge of things like babies left in wicker baskets. We pretended that these discussions were normal; I was reminded of the times when, as a child and a stutterer, I was unable to get a word out, and Dad had said it, to get me going, knowing I could deal with a sentence already under way. Now our roles and problems were reversed. Whereas I had been unable to verbally launch thoughts, and listened to my father do it for me, now he could not finish one and allowed his son to fill in words that offered at least the guise of a conclusion, and some comfort.

The last time I had depended upon my father had been at my wedding, sixteen years before. This event — I was only twenty-three at the time — followed an undistinguished college career and a year's writing fellowship at Stanford University, after I graduated from Southwestern, awarded for a novel I had begun in Memphis based on my river experiences. The winning of a fellowship by me was unexpected at home, and disconcerted people in different ways, among them myself, my parents, my friends, the draft board, and some Southwestern professors. It served as a true, unqualified savior, that rare, demonstrably precious event that still hangs in recollected western light, infused with the touch of the cold Pacific, the smell of blooming acacia, and a sense of infinite possibility.

California had absolutely nothing to do with home. A year after leaving I had briefly returned to Memphis with the girl I was to marry, a tall, red-headed Yankee named Penny Brennan, who also happened to be Catholic. We had nothing in common except the fact that we were elementally, imperviously in love. Her warmth and forbearance could have qualified her as southern; my mother acknowledged that Penny was not just attractive but also, in that distant place — Long Island — she considered home, surely belonged to the right people. Dad overlooked her religion and origins for the simple reason that he liked her, and he remained forever struck by the fact that I had chosen so well so far from Memphis. On the day Penny and I left for New York, he told me, "You're very lucky."

Up north, I proved less adept at acculturation than Penny had in Memphis. I was prone to drink too much and think it didn't matter; that I had written a short novel made even less of an impression there than it had at home. But my fiancée's father, a wise lawyer, knew a done deal when he saw one, and Penny and I were married in a suburban cathedral in September 1964.

After the ceremony everyone gathered at the country club, where Mom took me into the cloakroom to practice the waltz before I had to perform it, and my smiling wife, in her white gown, held me up through this trial, too. My cousin from Memphis played a protest song on the guitar, a reminder that the world was coming apart. At one point my father-in-law said to me, "Jim, there are a number of people drinking heavily at the bar."

Ralph, up from Chapel Hill, Rughead, Bink, who had been in love with Kit, my brother Frank, my cousin, and some other southerners formed an island beyond the promontory of wedding cake, across a sea of tablecloths and champagne flutes filled by waiters in a hurry. I wanted to tell him that was the way it was done. Then Dad stood up in front of all those strangers, in a place as foreign to him as any, and in a strong voice offered a toast that ended with the words "May the wind be always at their backs."

Penny and I returned to California, because that is where we had met, confident as only twenty-three-year-olds can be. We moved into the dining room of what had once been a grand house on Ashbury Street, cobbled into apartments, when the Haight was just a colorful lower-middle-class neighborhood and the Summer of Love lay a few years in the future. Penny was pregnant, an outcome of our two-month honeymoon in Mexico, living out of a secondhand Volkswagen given to us by her parents. She got a job with the phone company and I worked in a bookstore on Market Street. In the mornings I tried to write, and overhead, a cadaverous student from San Francisco State and his girlfriend feigned violent lovemaking while some of the Haight's thousand cats did the real thing up and down the once majestic staircase. We were in that transition from student to something else that in America can last for years, producing mostly dreams and offspring. I remained attached to Memphis by a temporal string of obligation and vague desire, a yoyo brought up short by news from there, dangled, drawn up again while talking to people about origins, or the South, by some association in what I was reading, by dreams. Each time the string got a little longer.

When my beautiful, fierce-looking son, Brennan, was born, I felt touched by a generational, continent-spanning importance; I already knew my child would be a boy, not because they had tests in those days but because my father had told me, with absolute authority, that Conaways were incapable of producing girls. I was also stricken with the absence of a job and the frightening prospect of real, rather than imagined, fatherhood. My novel had not been accepted for publication and I was forced to look for employment in the only field I could think of, journalism.

We moved to New Orleans where, thanks to Uncle Frank, I had been promised a tryout on the *Times-Picayune*. Suddenly I was providing, a strange and satisfying experience. As a cub reporter I rode the trolley down St. Charles to an institution that made the *Commercial Appeal* seem downright enterprising; later, as a crime reporter, I took the bus through the Dryades Street slums to the police station, past black faces and white touched with open, sweet corruption I had not encountered before. New Orleans may have been southern, but compared to Memphis it was another universe. My parents visited us there, and in Dad I saw a response to New Orleans's glad licentiousness and love of eating akin to my own. The façades of houses in the French Quarter and in the Garden District suggested a rich inner life; the memory of those in Overton Park and Chickasaw Gardens seemed deprived by comparison — one my father would never make.

A year and a half after moving to New Orleans, on the eve of Mardi Gras, Penny, Brennan, and I boarded a train for New York, bound ultimately for Europe. We had money saved for a few months but stayed four years, living what sounds like the expatriate idyll out of a novel but still marginally possible in places like Positano and Rome. Ours was an existence deprived of the known and secure, although the deprivation had its moments. I found a job on a rip-and-print English-language daily, the *Rome Daily American*, where my compatriots and some Englishmen performed every task, from editing to page makeup, drinking coffee brought continually from the café down the Via Dandolo and occasionally sleeping on the desks. My little nuclear family could almost live on the forty-nine dollars a week I was paid; we drank Frascati in refillable jugs, ate fungi the size of hamburgers sautéed in olive oil, bought oranges and tomatoes from reefs of produce in the clamorous Piazza San Cosimato, and fended off too much thinking about the future.

That is another story. In the midst of it I sometimes wondered what my parents would think of our acquaintances in the sub-basement of the movie industry — actors, directors, technicians, and dubbers drawn to the capital of the spaghetti western — and of those Europeans we considered friends although we could barely communicate with them. My mother disapproved of the aspiring American writers, mostly southerners, that I described to her in my letters. We would all gather like exiled White Russians over *granita* in Tre Scalini, and one of them would joke, when departing, "I'll see you in Memphis" — Memphis being the last place on earth we were likely to meet.

Dad, never much of a letter writer, stopped entirely. I knew that his business had improved, and his life. He had not gotten the engineer son he so wanted, his last chance, Dan, having turned to advertising, but they did things together as grown-ups that neither Frank nor I had done with my father. They played golf and attended professional matches at Colonial Country Club that would have been beyond consideration in less flush times; when traveling around the South, Dad searched for "coarse-ground grits," a symbol for him of good southern fare that was disappearing, along with other regional treasures, and of some leisure. Over the years I heard a lot about coarse-ground grits.

Dad seemed, by proxy, to have found contentment. He was frozen in my mind in that comfortable, indeterminate midlife pose common to the thinking of children with children of their own, who want some assurance that everything is all right at the top of the generational chain. My son had begun to talk in Italy, something my father would not hear; Brennan had no notion of grandparents or of family beyond my wife and me. All that could be rectified, I told myself, in time. But, years later, when Dad said to me, without rancor, "We weren't around for your trials and triumphs," I felt a wash of regret.

That winter, Penny, Brennan, and I spent in Switzerland, living on the third floor of a farmhouse with a view of the Vaudois Alps. We skied through brilliant afternoons, untrammeled by considerations other than the cost of *rosti* and the slightly effervescent white wine; at night, in bed, we listened to cows on the ground floor stamping their feet and blowing clouds of steam. I sold a magazine article — about New Orleans, not Italy or Switzerland. We had sufficient money to last until summer, when I would look for work on another English-language daily, in Paris, Athens, or Madrid. It was unrealistic and probably irresponsible, but knowing that didn't help abandon the illusion. Sometimes at four in the morning, ascending with the sounds of bovine unrest, would come suspicions of doom. Memphis, home, my father were part of them — the broad facet of the expatriate's willed, comfortable unreality, unassailable for the moment by place, language, even by the past.

One afternoon, driving our little two-cylinder car down the mountain, I picked up a hitchhiker, a Swiss, who asked me where I lived. I said, "Château d'Oex," and he said, "No, I mean where is your *home?*" I couldn't bring myself to say the word.

The diagnosis of Dad's problem, when it finally came, was inconclusive. My mother, my brothers, and I had discussed the disease then coming into public prominence and first identified, at about the time my father had been born, by a German physician, Alzheimer. None of us wanted to say the name, as if to do so was to invoke its awful power, its sibilant, fatal perniciousness. Alzheimer's was difficult to identify, we were told. The new family physician pointed out that Dad was old and that old people forget things. The doctor had that maddening air of the authority who has seen it all and seeks to reassure through pleasant condescension. His presumptuous, unearned fatalism angered me — this was *my* father we were talking about — but the psychiatrist was far worse.

I discussed the possibility with a colleague in Washington, a writer on problems of the aging, that my father was merely depressed. Physical ailments, the absence of his children, the deaths of old friends and relatives could possibly have left him hesitant and unsure, a recognized cause of mental distress in the elderly. The Conaways all seized the notion that if Dad could be cheered, perhaps with the aid of good American pharmacopoeia, his mental lapses and conversational fugues would slip away. From Washington I talked by telephone to a recommended psychiatrist in Memphis and when home took Dad to see him. The psychiatrist wore a gold bracelet that seemed incongruous on his plump, hairy wrist, and had an air of professional disdain for such a mundane subject as old persons, despite the fact that he trafficked in them. He insisted upon examining Dad alone, asked him to state the date and to count backward from one hundred, neither of which Dad could do. I was called in, and the psychiatrist, in front of Dad, proclaimed, "Dementia."

Dad and I went to a fast-food emporium afterward. The old feelings of helplessness and Memphian inevitability were enhanced by the jaundiced sun cutting up Union Avenue; Dad didn't know exactly what had been decided, only that it wasn't good and that he had been diminished. This didn't affect his appetite. Throughout most of his illness he ate an astonishing amount of food — fried chicken, tacos, roast beef, sweet potatoes, grits, tomato aspic, and lemon meringue pie — with increasing indifference to the table manners that had once been so important.

The ailment continued to defy naming until the naming was irrelevant, the course self-determining and clear enough. On subsequent visits to Memphis, my brothers and I shot pool with Dad. For years we had done this together; Dad was still the best. We watched him clean the table with displays of his beautiful follow-through. Dad disregarded the colors and numbers on the balls now, sinking the cue ball off the eight and the eight off the eleven and so on, until he lost interest, and we started the game all over again.

At the house, when I said I was going to take a shower, Dad told me, "Don't forget a spoon."

Sometimes, in the evening, he would come and stand in the middle of the living room and say to my mother, "Honey, let's go home."

"Connie, we *are* home."

He grew confused, exasperated. He didn't know what he meant, but we did. Dad wasn't talking about this rancher with its glass wall; he wasn't talking about the gray stone edifice in Overton Park where he had grown up. He was talking about the brick bungalow on Highland Avenue that was, the last time I had seen it, a bunch of boards and bricks collapsed into the cellar hole.

19

THAT PEOPLE we love die is basically unacceptable. The inevitability is fended off with the dual weapons of unelapsed time and dim possibility; we deceive ourselves into believing that life will go on, even as we acknowledge the deception.

I had learned of Jack's death when living in California and had felt both sadness and surprise. Also an instinctive relief, as if a symbolic impediment had been removed from my mother's life. I say symbolic because in reality Jack had ceased to be a factor years before, relegated to the little house on the wrong side of the tracks, a colorful, unorthodox presence who had, in his way, made the most of things. He had long white hair by then, and clattery false teeth. He couldn't hear the trains coupling less than a mile away. I like to think he could feel the vibrations and each time imagined quail bursting from cover somewhere in those seamless southern states.

My grandmother was expected to *live* after that, as if the removal of the rake from her life — one she happened to love — would transform her from an old woman into something else. She did travel a bit, and played with her great-grandson, Brennan, in New Orleans before we took him off for Europe. Her life had never been totally dependent upon another person, Jack included. You could say his dying left her unencumbered to be what she had always been: bright, generous, un-ownable, reader of Kipling, conjugator of Latin verbs fifty years after apprehending them, and irreplaceable.

Dodo died a few years after that and was buried next to my grandfather, not Jack, in Memorial Cemetery. I flew in for the ceremony. Dodo was spoken over by a young Methodist preacher whose words constricted my throat as soon as he began; he didn't like to think of Dodo going away, he said, and neither did I, reminded as I was of departures long past. The preacher said he preferred to think of Dodo arriving. "Over there, they're watching her ship on the horizon. They're saying, 'Here she comes! Here she comes!'"

I associate Dodo's dying with two earlier events. Part of the equation would have bothered her, had she heard it. Both associations may be illogical, but for me they are entwined: the final demise of *Hambone*, and that other death, the most signal one in Memphis's long, often unhappy history. We learned of it while still in Switzerland, in the spring of 1968, when Penny and I went for tea to the chalet of English friends. Wildflowers partitioned the hillside in bright sunshine; our host got out of his lawn chair and walked toward us too quickly. There is something in bad news that enhances the setting. Inconsequentials are burned into the larger text: the man's gesture, his waxed, wing-commander mustache, the precise way he said, "Have you heard? Martin Luther King's been shot in Memphis."

Images collide here, out of time. Maid and yard boy cavorting on soiled ticking in the "servants' quarters." An old man lifting me out of his dilapidated pickup, saying, "This ain't Miss'ippi." A Coke bottle thrown from a car that arches against the sky and disintegrates amidst the spokes of a bicycle ridden by an elaborately indifferent black teenager. Those dark figures running with their bundled clothes along the edge of the MCC golf course one hot summer's night.

It had taken the prolonged absence from the South and a catastrophe like King's murder to get me interested in Memphis in a way that transcended fiction and family. Over the next two years, before going back to confront the place, I read Woodward's *The Burden of Southern History,* Cash's *The Mind of the South,* Key's *Southern Politics,* and other books. Under the dire familiarity of home, I realized, lay some pretty interesting stuff. One book, *The Biography of a River Town,* written by a former Memphian and historian named Gerald Capers, reminded me that as a child I had heard Capers's name spoken and had seen his photograph in the newspaper. Memphians wanted Capers's hide then for daring to criticize Memphis and emphasizing its watery, opportunistic, transient past.

The Mississippi River, drawn from a million square miles of continent, was Memphis's salient feature, and yet the city turned its back on it. When I was growing up, the river was celebrated not as a fount of life but as a fairy-tale connection to a mealy-mouthed version of the old South and abhorred in reality as dirty and déclassé. We learned that in the 1500s Hernando de Soto's men ceremonially eased the explorer's body into the river's muddy sarcophagus but not that the lower Chickasaw bluff had been home to ragged soldiers left over from the War of 1812 and their Indian women who grew corn and sunflowers and hunted buffalo there. Even then a few prominent men living elsewhere dreamed of plats, to be sold for a fortune if they could get clear title to land that wasn't theirs.

One of them, Andrew Jackson, acting for the United States, bullied the Chickasaw Indians — our staunch allies against the French — out of roughly seven million acres between the Mississippi and Tennessee rivers, offering only four and a half cents an acre and essentially robbing them. He and his friends — James Winchester, a general and war hero, and John Overton, a former justice of the state supreme court — had a bogus claim to five thousand acres on the bluff which Jackson's deal legitimized. They named their nonexistent city after the one on the Nile.

It was a dismal river hamlet whose early citizens dealt in whatever moved by flatboat and survived disease, gunfights, and the wholesale consumption of whiskey. The Civil War was never a convincing cause in this "Charleston of the West" where, in 1862, five Union ironclads rammed and destroyed a small Confederate fleet on the river. The Memphians capitulated and were soon trading with both sides. Unlike most southern cities, Memphis grew inordinately during Reconstruction, when thousands of freedmen were drawn to it. Nativism had been more virulent among whites than antiblack sentiment before the war; after it, practical racism took over.

Poverty and violence strained the social fabric, and then in 1878 a yellow fever epidemic decimated the poor Irish and drove the German immigrants north to St. Louis, depriving Memphis of diverse, colorful elements. Government corruption and abiding squalor threw Memphis into bankruptcy, to be owned by New York bondholders. Until the early years of this century the city was run by that paragon of fiscal responsibility, the Tennessee state legislature. Still tough, Memphis saw its earlier settlers and small "nobility" replaced by rural outlanders more interested in displays of morality and a good sewer system than in a theater.

Mark Twain praised Memphis in *Life on the Mississippi* for assisting the victims of the steamboat explosion that killed his younger brother. "Many a disaster . . . had happened near her doors, and she was experienced, and above all other cities on the river, in the gracious office of the Good Samaritan." But Faulkner viewed Memphis primarily as a place to obtain booze. In "The Bear," Major de Spain and McCaslin send Boon and the boy, Ike, to Memphis to buy whiskey so the hunt can continue in Mississippi. (Boon gets hopelessly drunk.) In *Sanctuary*, the metaphor for Memphis is a brothel: "From the bluff, beyond a line of office buildings terraced sharply against the sunfilled sky, came a sound of traffic . . . Popeye drew up before one of the dingy three-storey houses," where the madam, Miss Reba, boasts, "'I've had some of the biggest men in Memphis right here in this house, bankers, lawyers, doctors — all of them.'" No wonder Memphis's many boosters never claimed serious kinship with Faulkner.

Two bullet holes marring the slab of glass near the spot where Martin Luther King fell weren't associated with that event. "You know how those things happen," said the brother of the manager of the Lorraine Motel as he unlocked the door to the shrine hung with a heart-shaped arrangement of yellow plastic flowers. It was 1970, and I was in Memphis for the first time since the murder, armed with a magazine assignment. By now I was a professional writer with a published novel to my credit and another book in progress; what drew me most strongly was the prospect of discovering, as an adult, how Memphis worked.

The marble plaque in the motel window bore the quotation from Genesis: "They said to one another, behold, here cometh the dreamer . . . Let us slay him . . . and we shall see what shall become of his dreams." Inside, preserved under glass, were the dishes from which King ate his last meal, the bedspread in which he was wrapped before being taken to the hospital, and an altar supporting the *Home Bible for Family Reading*, open to the prophets.

A few blocks to the north I found what was left of Beale Street. The old First Baptist Church dominated a razed plain east of Hernando Street that had been crowded with ramshackle houses sporting elaborate unpainted latticework the last time I had seen it. The restaurants — Red Johnny's and the Green Castle — were gone, too, and so were the Elks and Victory clubs. Lansky Brothers was still there, the same pegged pants in the window. Elvis still dropped by, according to a salesman, to pick up the occasional crushed velvet ensemble, but the man looked lonely.

Saplings had been planted in Handy Park and the bronze statue of the man put up. Both sides of Beale between Second and Fourth streets had been declared part of a national historic monument. The Memphis Housing Authority planned to incorporate it into its Beale Street Urban Renewal Project and to create a "Blue Light District," a shopping and entertainment plaza. Beale Street was being reinvented.

My enthusiasm for discovering the "real" Memphis led me to a cop, a city councilman, a founder of Holiday Inn, a trade unionist, a Chamber of Commerce publicist, the president of a black college, and members of the local contingent of the National Committee to Combat Fascism. I even talked to the president of the Junior League. The diminutive woman who headed Memphis's chapter of the National Association for the Advancement of Colored People told me, "The soul of Memphis hasn't changed in fifty years. As far as furthering the goals of Martin Luther King, I can't point to a single direct result of his death." Schools were integrated, she added, but black students were excluded from athletics and cheerleading. "Blacks are barred from churches — eleven o'clock on Sunday morning is still the most segregated hour in town."

But there were changes in 1970, and not all of them had to do with race. You could get a mixed drink now in Memphis without belonging to a club. Some graduates of Memphis University School, the "right" young Turks empowered with family money, had bought up near-derelict stores in midtown and created a bright social and alcoholic nexus there named, arbitrarily, Overton Square. It included a TGI Friday's and the Bombay Bicycle Shop, where businessmen not much older than I played backgammon and displayed their gold Rolexes. Red-white-and-blue saddle oxfords were the badge, I learned, of a local phenomenon known as the bond daddy, one of whom explained what he did for a living: "You call up a credit union in some little town and say, 'I got some securities here, all gov'mint-backed, paying twelve percent interest. Why don't you buy some?' You don't tell him the rate will go down if interest rates rise, which they do. Then you call him back and say, 'We've got a little problem with those bonds. They're down to nine percent and may go further. Why don't we cut our losses and buy into this new issue, one hunnert percent gov'mint-backed, that's paying ten and a half?' Later, you move on to the savings and loans. You call up this little bank down in Hernando, disguise your voice, and tell some old boy you're looking to buy whatever it is you really want to sell him. The next day you call him back and say in your normal voice, 'I got these bonds for sale, one hunnert percent gov'mint-backed . . .'"

Most bond daddies seemed to be headed either for prison or for Houston. I was amazed at the sight of ordinary people, some of whom I had known, getting rich through these and other schemes, rather than the august pursuit of cotton or residential real estate. Meanwhile other people were going crazy. Three political assassinations in half a dozen years and the war in Vietnam had loosed in the country a general, low-level desperation, but Memphis had its own brand, often related to alcohol. Money didn't seem to help. A friend of mine who had attended Southwestern, the son of a prosperous car dealer, spent some of his inheritance on flights around the United States. He would arrive in the Los Angeles airport, change his mind about where he wanted to be, and fly to Chicago. Once there, he would change his mind again and fly to New Orleans. Back home in Memphis, peeved at the ordinariness of life, he would attack the latest model of the car provided by his father's enterprise. Innumerable devastated dashboards were replaced by that long-suffering dealership. He later committed suicide.

No less than three of my friends from Southwestern did or would do the same. One, a near-brilliant philosophy student who should have taught but instead sold light fixtures in bulk, a Tau alumnus with no extraordinary appetite for alcohol by Memphis's standards, stood at the window of his girlfriend's apartment, in front of a small crowd, and shot himself through the head.

Some of the people I interviewed in Memphis weren't happy to see me. Although many didn't know I was a local, my accent might have reassured them. But the fact that I represented an "outside" publication did not. The city had raised a reported four million dollars to "sell" Memphis to a disapproving world and had apparently failed. A commissioned study of the social and economic health of Memphis had suggested that the problems were old and intractable, related to a legacy of political bossism and resistance to change. The report itself was suppressed by tacit agreement among Chamber of Commerce members, politicians, and the press — the old troika.

I ended up in City Hall, where once a week the mayor, heir to a lucrative laundry business, held court. He wore a button-down shirt but no jacket. Wide-set, unfocused eyes; shades of Valentino in the slick black hair. The garbagemen's strike two years before and the aftermath of King's murder had been his to deal with, and they had left him testy. He had just returned from a trip to New York, where he had gone armed with stuffed catfish glued to cypress planks, presents for corporate leaders, part of an unsuccessful attempt to lure jobs to Memphis.

The mayor started the session by refusing to arrange a meeting with the governor for a man in the audience, saying, "I'm not a hack politician." He refused to donate a plastic flower to the Southside Baptist Church ("It would look like I was trying to buy votes"). He refused a request for the installation of a traffic light from a man chewing a damp cigar. "Danny Thomas asked me to have a light put in at the foot of the bridge," the mayor said, "and I didn't even do that."

Displeased, the man with the cigar stood up. He dragged a foot across the new carpet, said, "If I had some of this in my house, I'd think I was in heaven," and headed for the door.

The mayor overtook him, grasped his hand and began to saw. "I want you to feel free to come on down here any Thursday you like."

Nervous, feeling more like nine years old than twenty-nine, recognizing that I was touching old wounds, I asked the mayor for his opinion of the influence on Memphis of the death of Martin Luther King. His bodyguard looked at me in an unpleasant way, scratching his biceps; the mayor waited a full ten seconds before saying, through clenched teeth, "I don't *have* any opinion."

The article I wrote, for *The Atlantic*, was not particularly critical, though it did not flatter Memphis. I heard that my uncle disliked it, and so did my father. Still strong of mind in those days, Dad resented the fact that the world blamed his city for King's murder more than he did the murder itself, not a happy admission for me to make, but one essential to understanding a particular, defensive view. "You were raised here," Dad said when next I talked to him on the telephone. "You should have done better by us."

I didn't feel enlightened by the experience, nor triumphant. I felt squelched. The implication was that what Memphians did or didn't do, thought or didn't think, was none of my or any other outsider's business — the same reaction my grandfather probably encountered after drawing his anti-Klan cartoon back in the twenties. Life entails difficulties for which no one is accountable. Pressures produce sometimes tragic results, but that doesn't mean anything is *wrong*. To suggest otherwise is to be guilty of disloyalty.

20

MONEY BECAME a problem for my parents. Though Dad's ailment had a name, it remained difficult to prove and impossible to cure, and so various government entities, including the one for helping veterans, couldn't be induced to help him. The maid still showed up once a week, but it fell to my mother, also in her seventies, to care for an invalid who increasingly forgot names, hid the mail, shuffled and sometimes stumbled, defied the most potent sleeping pills, dribbled his food, railed at his wife for the loss of his right to drive and other frustrations, and even threatened to hit her if his increasingly phantasmagoric landscape didn't hold still.

Yet she refused to entomb him in a nursing home. They owned the house but could not afford it and permanent help, and buying a smaller place, to free up money, couldn't be discussed calmly. The suggestion that they consider moving to midtown, into a relatively inexpensive, clean, but aging duplex, awakened in her the old fear of the wrong neighborhood. She described this one as "decadent" and talked of largely nonexistent excess equity, part of the money that came from selling Dad's business. Some of this had been invested in a movie-making company with Goldie Hawn in tow that was supposed to make my parents rich, sold to them by another of those specialists in assisting the aged, but did not. This decision, and others related to keeping up standards rather than to necessity, generated lucre-driven arguments I will always regret.

These occurred face to face when I was home, over the telephone when I wasn't. Budgets were meticulously drawn up and then ignored. That I and Frank lived far away in Yankeeland wasn't the reason we lacked real influence; our brother Dan lived in Memphis, across town, but couldn't effect these hard decisions either. Mom had never been comfortable with advice and now developed an enameled independence that in a curious way kept her going. All her life she had relied indirectly on the presence of a man, first her father, then mine; her mental and physical ailments, real and otherwise, had in part, I am sure, grown out of her unsettled relationships with both. Still, she measured possibility by their prospects and their attitudes toward her; she saw herself both enhanced and limited by them. Now suddenly there were no alternatives to herself and her single, obvious, unhappy future, and she dealt with it in a way that I would not have thought possible.

Dad's unyielding brand of dementia would have been a match for a dispassionate professional nurse. His — my mother — was ardent about him, which increased her psychological load proportionately. But Mom's resolve stiffened in opposition to the illness. This toughness exasperated her sons but also moved us. She managed to laugh at some of the absurdities, like Dad's inclination to fall in love with women he encountered. When I took him to the local Alzheimer's clinic, and spent a few minutes talking to the woman who ran it, Dad offered in a friendly way to knock me down if I didn't stop. He thought I should get on with the employment, whatever it might be, that was supposed to occupy a man my age on a weekday morning, and leave the field to him.

My "work" had always been something of a mystery to Dad. For most of my professional life I had been what is known as a freelance writer, and was one again; he had respected this, when he was capable, not because he valued writing but because the task was demanding and I had stuck with it. He had read in all but I suspect hadn't finished any of my books; what he cared about in them and in the articles wasn't the style or even the subject so much as the risks of compilation, financial and emotional. What I did for a living was a kind of entrepreneurial dare in Dad's eyes, not unlike that of an undegreed engineer confident he would always find another building to air-condition.

He had told me, not too many years before, "You've burned your bridges." I was surprised by the modicum of admiration in his voice. Dad had not burned his bridges, valuing as he did the interconnections among family, friends, and place — particularly if that place was Memphis. But the fact that I had moved from project to project, from other place to other place, and had prospered, impressed him.

On that occasion he had said something else that both surprised and pleased me: "You're a man." This was no grand proclamation, more an acknowledgment, casual and a shade reluctant, that he seemed to want on the record. What he meant, I think, was that I had proven to be an individual, whatever my choices. I was independent, when most men answered directly to others. By that time much of what I had learned from my father had been put to uses he never envisioned, or discounted. My children — as a Conaway I had proven capable, after all, of producing two fine daughters, in addition to my son — and my wife were important elements in Dad's appraisal of what I had become, but not decisive. He didn't sympathize with a lot of what I thought and wrote, or with where we lived, but the wheres and wherebys of our life had been largely our own doing, and that had value in his eyes.

The end surprised me — us — as I suppose it had to, and immediately took on the guise of inevitability. Dan called one day and said, "Mom's had a stroke," and all the visions of the unfolding future in Memphis collapsed, as she had, on the lawn next to the flower bed. She would have died but for the black man, Hargis, who worked occasionally for my parents and who found Mom and set the rescue in motion. The assumption that she would survive my father and move on, as women seemed to do, to a happier, if increasingly fragile, solitude suddenly seemed preposterous, even criminal. We had neglected to appreciate the obvious — that Mom was living under unacceptable demands — and to force on her the decision to have my father committed.

Now she was herself a victim of his illness, unconscious and waiting for an operation that was extremely grave. The clinical term for her stroke was aneurysm, a ballooning of a blood vessel in the brain, a hideous, vivid abstraction that usually kills outright. It didn't kill my mother. Dan had driven her to the hospital; neither he nor she knew the seriousness of what had happened. Although her pain must have been terrible, she attempted to chat, valuing as always the need for sociability, responding to real rather than imagined trouble with courage that put everything else to rest.

Because of the confusion, Dad had to spend that night alone. The next morning he managed to telephone me in Washington. Like a child, he asked, "Where is everybody?"

My brothers and I converged in an antic knot of grief and uncertainty; the priorities sorted themselves out. My mother survived the surgery, but in what condition we wouldn't know for weeks, maybe months. She lay in the Baptist Hospital enwombed in tubes and bandages, unrecognizable. My father didn't know what had happened to her, or even which part of her to address, but he talked to her without interruption when there, as if she were awake and not in a coma, and as soon as we got him home again would say, "Let's go see Kathryn."

We visited three times a day with a man who barely knew us and whose reason for being at the hospital faded in and out of an already vertiginous reality. His doctor, when he heard about it, expressed consternation at these jaunts. That three grown sons would acquiesce in the irrational demands of their failing father seems unlikely and maybe excessive to me, too, and remains something for which I am profoundly grateful.

Between visits, Frank, Dan, and I toured Memphis's nursing homes, putting aside whatever differences we had over money and precedents, stiff-arming the dire associations, until we found one in the eastern sector of the city that had an aura of suburban light missing from the place where Dad's mother, aunt, and uncle had ended up. It was called Bright Glade.

The night before we moved him, we all got a little drunk — we brothers, and Frank's oldest son, Danny, who had also flown in from New York. And, of course, Dad. This time alcohol served a purpose beyond the reach of sentiment or drugs that was undeniably good. Dad's drinking days had ended, but as we sat around the table he sipped a little wine, and an amazing thing happened: he shed, however briefly, the lost look of the terminally deranged and put on the old, sweet insouciance of the perennial party boy. He might not have known our names but he did know that he belonged to us; he teased, and cussed a bit, and even threw — gingerly — a piece of cutlery. Boys, even three generations of them in the midst of domestic disaster, were supposed to be cutups, dangerous but adorable. He had been viewed that way as a child, and by my mother, too; in this brief, boozy epiphany I glimpsed all that had been bundled down to me and my brothers and our children, and wondered what place on the planet could possibly replicate such a curious blend of love and delusion.

At Bright Glade, America's actuarial bias lay starkly exposed in the foyer. One man and many women sat in wheelchairs, all facing the door like a school of steelhead waiting for the river to rise. We hung my mother's oil paintings on the walls of Dad's room; one was of the house outside Tucson where my parents had spent that glorious year in the thirties. But Dad wasn't happy with his new digs. The following day we received a call from the home's director, telling us that Dad had attempted to walk out and, when detained, had threatened to strike the attendant. I inferred that Dad had used the racial epithet once so common in Memphis, and I hurried back to Bright Glade and lectured my father, who listened in perplexity, sitting in the stuffed chair we had hauled over from the house. I was afraid the staff would lose patience with and neglect him, but I was wrong. In my fumbling attempt to apologize to them for his conduct I must have lost my composure; a large black woman took my hand sympathetically, as if I were the patient and she was saying that all this discord and anxiety is transitory and ultimately insignificant.

My mother emerged from the hospital but, as we feared, totally dependent. Dan found a place for her in St. Peter's, next door to the orphanage, with facilities for dealing with the aged and the damaged. Hers had been to the right side of the brain, which lent her speech, when she finally began to speak again, a slow, curious formality. When one of us held the door open for her wheelchair, Mom gazed up and said, in perfect seriousness, "Chivalry is not dead."

She spent long minutes examining the faces of those who came to see her, relieved at last of the necessity of entertaining. She would whisper a name when it suited her, or say nothing at all. Our initial hope that she might eventually be taken out of St. Peter's and ensconced in some replication of her former life, with an attendant, slipped away in the incremental reports of doctor and therapist.

Mom's hair had been shorn for the operation; it returned a steel gray streaked with white, past needing the attention and agents that had kept it close to its youthful color. The surgery had left its physical impression, too, a reminder both of the pain she must have undergone beforehand and the daring of such a radical procedure. Her paralyzed left side caused her to list in her wheelchair, so that visiting with Mom involved a more or less constant bolstering of her and a maneuvering to her right so she could keep us in view. The transformation had starkly revealed to me the precariousness of what we consider normal, and the way in which calamity telescopes time, obliterating easeful transitions and bringing us face to face in an instant with truths we have known all along. Past omissions roll back on you when it's too late to do anything about them.

Once I went to visit Mom in the morning before the attendants had gotten her up and into her wheelchair. She lay inside the bed's guardrail, embroiled in covers. She was not asleep, however, and when I touched her, she asked, "Who am I?"

I said, "You're Kathryn Alley Conaway, daughter of Nona and J. P. Alley, wife of Connie, mother of Frank, Jim, and Danny."

That seemed to help. We all knew by then that Mom had essentially done away with distinctions of time, that her father and mother, sister and brothers, children, friends, doctors, preachers, and Hargis all swam in a multigenerational pool, connected, friendly, unimpaired by the years. This allowed her direct access to people and moments once lost, to things she valued or had grieved for — a renewal of sorts. Her existence was not happy, but for once there was no past to deal with, no expectations.

21

DURING THE YEAR that Dad lived at Bright Glade, I saw him only a few times. He was almost always asleep, there in the foyer with the others. First they fed him with a spoon and then with a big plastic syringe. He continued to shrink. When awake, his eyes danced desperately. He had lost the ability to walk, and I, pushing his wheelchair along the outdoor path, would see him attempt to follow the flight of a jay, and try to envision life with a relentless mental strobe, each flickering image bearing no relation to what preceded or followed it. Once, for an instant, he recognized me, mouthed the words "I love you," and then he was off again, buffeted by interior winds that drove him beyond any imaginable shore. He died in his room there, Dan holding a hand that had grown thin and dry as cardboard.

The day of the funeral, Frank, Dan, and I went first to see our mother. She had not so far spoken of Dad, something we thought odd, since she had spoken of almost everyone else in the family. Now, without prompting or any possible knowledge of what had happened to my father, she said, "Connie's coming to the party."

That same day she told my brother, "They pronounced Daddy officially dead today."

I can't explain this. Whether prescience, a manifestation of some latent awareness on her part, or coincidence, it left us all wondering. About unsuspected links and what for want of a better phrase I will call the power of affection.

Dad's will was an old one, scribbled on graph paper. He had requested cremation and the spreading of his ashes on the surface of the Mississippi River, at a point of our choosing. The Coast Guard told us, when we inquired, that this was not permissible, but we decided to do it anyway. One bleak afternoon in spring the three of us boarded a houseboat piloted by a neighbor of Dan's and set out from the marina on Mud Island, at the foot of the city. Frank carried the small metal can containing Dad's ashes, Dad's name typed on a bit of paper taped to the snap-on lid. What Dad had hoped for, I think, when he wrote the will, was some accord among the three of us, and maybe even festivity. I had brought along a half pint of Jim Beam, a sentimental gesture, but at the last moment had left it under the seat of the car.

We headed upstream. In another month the river would rise above the levee on the Arkansas bank and spread away like an inland, caramel-colored sea. The current rode up the stone buttresses beneath the new bridge with its dramatic spans; we could feel the tug of that dark water.

Our pilot said, "Be sure the wind's behind you."

Frank removed the lid from the can and sprinkled some ashes; I and Dan took our turns. Each time a suggestion of smoke drifted aslant the river's surface, falling. Nothing was said. When the ashes were gone, Dan sank the tin; I tossed the lid. It floated my father's name briefly beneath the eye of the world.

*

A month after my father died, I dreamed that I saw a man walking with assurance along an empty airport corridor, carrying a hanging bag. It was Dad, thirty years younger, his hair thick on the sides, deep chestnut in color, his lean, muscular arms protruding from the rolled sleeves of his shirt with the old-fashioned pointed collars. I was surprised to see him there because he did not like to fly — flying was expensive and tended to take you to places where you would just as soon not be — and yet he was off, waving, through a dim, untended portal.

A year later, I dreamed I was in a distant city and wanted to leave, to get to a place where I had left something of significance. My inquiries made to the faceless person behind a cash register elicit no response. Across the street is parked a station wagon, red in the streaking rain; a clipboard on the seat suggests scheduling, imminent departure. A man sits on the passenger side. "Dad," I say, and he turns and smiles, the polished rims of his spectacles gathering the light. He wears the tan raincoat I know so well. He says, "Get in, son," with the friendly authority of a man who knows where he, where *we,* are going and is happy to provide deliverance and good company.

All my dreams were for a long time confused and brilliantly colored. People I knew and had known swam in a universal stream not unlike my mother's thoughts, undiminished by time: lustrous, almost tangible. One night I dreamed that Kit and I were together on one of those crowded Mississippi River party steamers that had floated the alcoholic excesses of Tau Delta Tau. We were both naked. The captain came to me and said, "Jim, you've got to make that speech," and I was on my way to the bandstand when I woke up.

Another time, after I had begun to write about the past, I dreamed of sitting in my room on Highland Avenue with my parents. Mom said, "Just give us time, we'll get this place cleaned up." Outside, beyond the window, the figure of a boy appeared, climbing the fence; with the terrible swiftness of a nightmare he became threatening and unspeakably malevolent. Afraid, determined to protect us, I rushed out to do battle and saw that the marauder was myself.

During a real visit to Memphis, I drank beer with Metcalf in Alex's, the last of the good old taverns. It had been injected with big-screen television and the relentless feed of professional sports but otherwise might have contained the oxygen we breathed in 1959. Talk turned to my fight of twenty-five years before, in the parking lot of the Whirlaway, and I felt all the stoppered anger of that event. I decided, in the remnant light of memory, to go out and find my antagonist of long ago and to formally avenge myself. "Too late," said Metcalf, and he was laughing. "He just had a triple bypass."

Sometimes I find myself, in the midst of someone else's assertion, thinking, "You're wrong about that." I sometimes see, when talking to my children, myself looking back at my father. I like to think that what I learned from him has been integrated in an entirely different person, that old fears and shortfalls have been absorbed and that the endurance of quirks from one generation to the next is a myth.

For some reason I chew the stems of my glasses, as he did. I am impatient. I sometimes feel ill suited to the notion of home, and when gone yearn for an immutable place where people and comforts, even foolish ones, endure.

In the breakup of Dad's incidentals I found myself in possession of his old Seabees belt buckle. I don't wear it much, but I do put on a fresh T-shirt when undertaking some manual task of a dwindling Saturday afternoon, far from Memphis. I think I am going about this casually, out of choice, but I know that others don't see it that way. They see a determined man assigned to action, not for violence but for the problems it poses, the primary one being that things tend to fall down and must be kept upright.

Two years after my father died, my brothers and I decided to move Mom from St. Peter's to a place out east. The decision was based upon financial need and what we thought was continuing care, but sentiment played a part, too. The new nursing home was just off Highland Avenue, a quarter mile from where we had lived. Although commerce had destroyed the block where our house had stood, that part of the street within view of Mom's new residence had retained its oaks and air of somnolent ease.

One afternoon in early autumn, while visiting, I wheeled her outside, a rare excursion since she was very frail now. Passers-by looked at us as if we reminded them of something they wanted to forget. I don't know if Mom realized how close she was to the spot where she had grown up, but I like to think she did. I had asked her not long before if she remembered Highland, and she had said, "We had a good time," and then, after a long pause, had added, "But we didn't know it."

Another time she had said, softly but insistently, "I am known."

This was part of an ongoing monologue about her accomplishments and the world's response to them. Her imagination sometimes got out of hand. She had claimed, among other things, that the *New York Times* described her as the greatest artist in the universe, and that she had been three times crowned Queen of England. But mostly Mom had talked about family — relatives engaged in ordinary activities with one another, often impossible in time but sure to her mind and thereby infused with reality as valid as any. It was a mother's reconciliation of impossibles, the granting of her and her people's fondest wishes, and a testament to the persistence of love through a bleak if widespread sort of decline. I had said, "Yes, Mom, you are known. You're famous."

That day she was beyond speech — she didn't have long to live — and her white hair seemed to burn in the angled sunlight. She blinked at the brightness but, I think, enjoyed access to real air. It was warm the way it is in Memphis in the fall, full of leaf smell, the humidity lifting. Ours was a one-sided conversation, but I felt comfortable with it, for once. I just talked about Highland Avenue, talked about home.